إذ أوى الفتية إلى الكهف فقالوا ربنا

ءاتنا من لدنك رحمة وهيئ لنا من أمرنا رشدا ۝

IN THE COMPANY OF THE QURAN

AN EXPLANATION OF
SURAH AL-KAHF

BY **FURHAN ZUBAIRI**

© 2025 FURHAN ZUBAIRI

All rights reserved. Aside from fair use, meaning a few pages or less for non-profit educational purposes, review, or scholarly citation, no part of this publication may be reproduced, stored in a retrieval system, or transmitted in any form or by any means, electronic, mechanical, photocopying, recording, or otherwise, without the prior permission of the Copyright owner. For permission requests, please write to the publisher at the address below.

Imam Ghazali publishing
USA – Malaysia – UK
info@imamghazali.co
www.imamghazali.co

BULK ORDERING INFORMATION: Special discounts are available on quantity purchases. For details, please contact the publisher.

The views, information, or opinions expressed are solely those of the author(s) and do not necessarily represent those of the publisher.

FIRST PUBLISHING, 2020
SECOND PUBLISHING, 2025

ISBN: 978-1-966329-25-1

Typeset in Lato, Nassim, and KFGQPC Uthmanic Script HAFS
Arabic Symbols: KFGQPC Arabic Symbols 01

Dedicated to my daughters Zainab, Hafsa, and Layla. May Allah make them companions of the Quran.

Contents

Revelation,
Belief & Disbelief

The Story of the Owner of
the Two Gardens

The Day of Judgement & the Severe
Consequences of Rejecting the Message

The Story of Mūsa عليه السلام
& al-Khaḍir

Revelation,
Belief & Disbelief Revisited

Transliteration & Pronunciation Key

Arabic Letter	Transliteration	Sound
ء	'	A slight catch in the breath, cutting slightly short the preceding syllable.
ا	*ā*	An elongated *a* as in *cat.*
ب	*b*	As in *best.*
ت	*t*	As in *ten.*
ث	*th*	As in *thin.*
ج	*j*	As in *jewel.*
ح	*ḥ*	Tensely breathed *h* sound made by dropping tongue into back of throat, forcing the air out.
خ	*kh*	Pronounced like the *ch* in Scottish *loch,* made by touching back of tongue to roof of mouth and forcing air out.
د	*d*	As in *depth.*
ذ	*dh*	A thicker *th* sound as in *the.*
ر	*r*	A rolled *r*, similar to Spanish.
ز	*z*	As in *zest.*
س	*s*	As in *seen.*
ش	*sh*	As in *sheer.*
ص	*ṣ*	A heavy *s* pronounced far back in the mouth with the mouth hollowed to produce full sound.
ض	*ḍ*	A heavy *d/dh* pronounced far back in the mouth with the mouth hollowed to produce a full sound.
ط	*ṭ*	A heavy *t* pronounced far back in the mouth with the mouth hollowed to produce a full sound.
ظ	*ẓ*	A heavy *dh* pronounced far back in the mouth with the mouth hollowed to produce a full sound.
ع	'	A guttural sound pronouned narrowing the throat.
غ	*gh*	Pronounced like a throaty French *r* with the mouth hallowed.
ف	*f*	As in *feel.*
ق	*q*	A guttural *q* sound made from the back of the throat with the mouth hallowed.
ك	*k*	As in *kit.*
ل	*l*	As in *lip.*
م	*m*	As in *melt.*
ن	*n*	As in *nest.*
ه	*h*	As in *hen.*

و	*w* (at the beg. of syllable)	As in *west*.
	ū (in the middle of syllable)	An elongated *oo* sound, as in *boo*.
ي	*y* (at beg. of syllable)	As in *yes*.
	ī (in the middle of syllable)	An elongated *ee* sound, as in *seen*.

Used following the mention of Allah, God, translated as, "Glorified and Exalted be He."

Used following the mention of the Prophet Muḥammad, translated as, "May God honor and protect him."

Used following the mention of any other prophet or Gabriel, translated as, "May God's protection be upon him."

Used following the mention of the Prophet Muḥammad's Companions, translated as, "May God be pleased with them."

Used following the mention of a male Companion of the Prophet Muḥammad, translated as, "May God be pleased with him."

Used following the mention of a female Companion of the Prophet Muḥammad, translated as, "May God be pleased with her."

Used following the mention of two Companions of the Prophet Muḥammad, translated as, "May God be pleased with them both."

Used following the mention of the major scholars of Islam, translated as, "May God have mercy on them."

Used following the mention of a major scholar of Islam, translated as, "May God have mercy on him."

INTRODUCTION

In the Name of Allah, the Most Merciful, the Very Merciful. All thanks and praise are due to Allah ﷻ, the Lord of the worlds, and may His blessings and protection be upon His last and final Messenger, Muḥammad ﷺ, his family, his companions, and those who follow them until the end of times.

عَـنْ أَبِي هُرَيْـرَةَ رَضِيَ اللهِ عَنْـهُ قَـالَ: قَـالَ رَسُـولُ اللهِ ﷺ: "مَـا اجْتَمَعَ قَـوْمٌ فِي بَيْـتٍ مِـنْ بُيُـوتِ اللهِ يَتْلُـونَ كِتَـابَ اللهِ، وَيَتَدَارَسُـونَهُ بَيْنَهُـمْ؛ إِلَّا نَزَلَـتْ عَلَيْهِـمْ السَّـكِينَةُ، وَغَشِـيَتْهُمْ الرَّحْمَـةُ، وَ حَفَتهُـمْ المَلَائِكَـةُ، وَذَكَرَهُـمْ اللهُ فِيمَـنْ عِنْدَهُ"

From Abū Hurairah ؓ who said that the Messenger of Allah ﷺ said, "A group of people does not gather in one of the houses of Allah, reciting the Book of Allah, and studying it together among themselves, except that tranquility descends upon them, mercy covers them, the Angels surround them, and Allah mentions them among those who are with Him."[1]

عَـنْ عُثْمَـانَ بْـنِ عَفَّـانَ رَضِيَ اللهِ عَنْـهُ قَـالَ: قَـالَ رَسُـولُ اللهِ ﷺ: "خَيْرُكُـمْ مَـنْ تَعَلَّـمَ الْقُـرْآنَ وَعَلَّمَـهُ"

1 Muslim, *k. al-dhikr wa al-duʿā wa al-tawbah wa al-istighfār, b. faḍl al-ijtimāʿ ʿalā tilāwah al-quran wa ʿalā al-dhikr,* 2699

From Uthmān ibn Affān ﷺ who said that the Messenger of Allah ﷺ said, "The best among you is the one who learns the Quran and teaches it."[2]

عَـنْ أَبِي هُرَيْـرَةَ، قَـالَ قَـالَ رَسُـولُ اللَّهِ ﷺ "مَـنْ سَـلَكَ طَرِيقًـا يَلْتَمِـسُ فِيـهِ عِلْمًـا سَـهَّلَ اللَّهُ لَهُ طَرِيقًـا إِلَى الْجَنَّـةِ"

From Abū Hurairah ﷺ who said that the Messenger of Allah ﷺ said, "Whoever takes a path to obtain knowledge, Allah makes the path to Paradise easy for him."[3]

Without a doubt the Quran is the most important book in the life of a Muslim. That is because the Quran is not simply a book; it is the divine uncreated speech of Allah ﷻ — His words revealed to the last and final Prophet and Messenger ﷺ. It is the last and final revelation sent for the guidance of humanity for all times and all places. It is our primary source of beliefs, rituals, ethics, morals, and laws in Islam. Our entire lives as Muslims revolve around the teachings of the Quran. Its words are so powerful, emotive, and effective that if they were to be revealed on a mountain, it would be humbled and burst apart out of the awe of Allah[4]. Its recitation, memorization, interpretation, understanding, teaching, and learning are all acts of worship that bring blessings and reward. These words are a source of light, guidance, cure, and mercy.

True love and respect for the Quran is expressed through reading it, understanding its message, and applying it to our lives. We use it as a source of guidance to navigate through the world and live a life that is pleasing to Allah ﷻ. It is literally our manual for life that we use to build a path towards the Divine. It is supposed to be our inspiration, encouragement, and the tool we use to deal with the challenges of life. It contains guidance for every single aspect of our lives: theological, spiritual, individual, familial, communal, economic, and political.

The primary objective of the Quran is for us to think, ponder, and reflect over its meanings. As Allah ﷻ tells us, "[This is] a blessed Book which

---

2 Bukhārī, *k. faḍā'il al-Quran, b. khayrukum man taʿallama al-quran wa ʿallamahu,* 5027

3 Tirmidhi, *k. al-ʿilm ʿan rasūlillah, b. mā jā'a fī faḍl al-ʿilm,* 2646

4 59:21

We have revealed to you, [O Muḥammad], that they might reflect upon its verses and that those of understanding would be reminded."[5] Blessed, this one-word description of the Quran, is actually very comprehensive. Every single aspect of the Quran is blessed: its words, meanings, style, stories, commands, and prohibitions. Its recitation, memorization, interpretation, learning, and teaching are all acts of worship that bring great amounts of reward and blessing.

Part of its blessings is that those who learn it and teach it to others are considered to be the best of people. For every single letter of the Quran that is recited, a person is rewarded with a good deed that is multiplied by ten. The Prophet ﷺ said, "Whoever recites a letter from the book of Allah, then for them is a good deed, and a good deed is multiplied by ten. I am not saying that *alif lām mīm* is one letter, but *alif* is a letter, *lām* is a letter, and *mīm* is a letter."[6] The Quran will intercede for its companion on the Day of Judgment. The Prophet ﷺ said, "Recite the Quran because it will come as an intercessor for its companion on the Day of Judgment."[7] Through the Quran, some nations are elevated while others are lowered.[8] From all of these narrations we can see that the simple act of reciting the Quran is full of blessings, reward, virtues, and mercy.

However, it's extremely important for us to understand and recognize that mere recitation and listening is not the purpose of the Quran. The main purpose or objective of reciting the Quran or listening to the Quran is to reflect, ponder, and think over its meanings, and more importantly, bring its guidance into our daily lives. When we come across a verse that has a command we're supposed to accept it and follow it. When we come across a prohibition, we stay away from it without complaint. When we come across a verse describing the mercy of Allah ﷻ, we should ask for that mercy and hope for it. When we come across a verse that threatens punishment, we should feel a sense of fear and seek protection from it.

The only way to contemplate and reflect over its words and meanings is to actually know what those words and meanings are, and that is learned through Tafsīr, the qualified explanation of the Quran. That is why learning

5 38:29

6 Tirmidhī, *k. faḍā'il al-qur'ān 'an rasūlillah*, 2910

7 Muslim, *k. salah al-musāfirīn, b. faḍl qirā'ah al-qur'ān wa sūrah al-baqarah*, 804

8 Muslim, *k. salah al-musāfirīn, b. faḍl man yaqūm bi al-qur'ān…*, 817

Tafsīr is considered to be an obligation upon every Muslim in varying degrees. One way to look at it is that the Quran is a treasure chest full of guidance and wisdom. The key to unlocking that chest is Tafsīr. Tafsīr is a tool that aids us in having a holistic understanding of the Quran allowing us to understand it correctly to extract guidance, lessons, morals, and reminders.

Based on a few narrations from the Prophet ﷺ, which I will mention later, one of the chapters of the Quran that we are encouraged to recite on a weekly basis is Sūrah[9] al-Kahf. It is a very common practice across the Muslim world to recite Sūrah al-Kahf on Fridays. This is a beautiful practice that helps strengthen one's relationship with the Quran and builds a culture of recitation. However, more important than simply reciting the Sūrah as a ritual is connecting with it emotionally, intellectually, spiritually, and trying our best to understand its message and apply its guidance into our daily lives.

With this thought in mind, I was blessed with the opportunity of teaching an explanation of Sūrah al-Kahf to the community at my local masjid, Dār al-Falāḥ, and at the Institute of Knowledge. The recordings can be found on the Institute of Knowledge YouTube channel. I thought it would be a good idea to organize the notes I used for those lectures into a publication exploring the meanings and lessons of Sūrah al-Kahf.

I am in no way, shape, or form a scholar of the Quran or qualified to do Tafsīr. I'm not saying that with some false sense of humility. In these lectures and this publication I am simply conveying what I have studied with my teachers and continue to read from various works of Tafsīr with my own clarification and insights. I have compiled this work using the following sources:

1. al-Tafsīr al-Munīr by the late Dr. Wahbah al-Zuḥaylī رحمه الله
2. Tafsīr ibn Kathīr
3. Tafsīr al-Qurṭubī
4. Tafsīr al-Jalālayn
5. Tafsīr al-Taḥrīr wa al-Tanwīr by the late ibn Āshūr
6. Fī Dhilāl al-Quran by the late Syed Qutb رحمه الله
7. Maārif al-Qurān by the late Mufti Muhḥmmad Shafī رحمه الله

I would like to thank all of those individuals who provided suggestions,

9 Literally meaning "a boundary", but is used to refer to a chapter of the Quran. It will be written as sūrah henceforth.

comments, improvements and took the time out of their busy schedules to edit this short work. May Allah ﷻ reward our IOK Seminary student Munir Eltal and and Seminary graduate Mudassir Mayet, continue to bless them, and increase them in knowledge. I would also like to thank Sr. Sara Bokker and my wife, Fatima Rangoonwala, for providing beneficial suggestions and editing the work.

I ask Allah ﷻ to bless this small effort and make it beneficial for those who read it. I ask Allah ﷻ to bless all of us with a strong relationship with the Quran so that we can engage it, ponder over its meanings, and bring its blessing into our lives. May Allah ﷻ shower His blessings and mercy upon His last and final messenger, Muḥammad ﷺ.

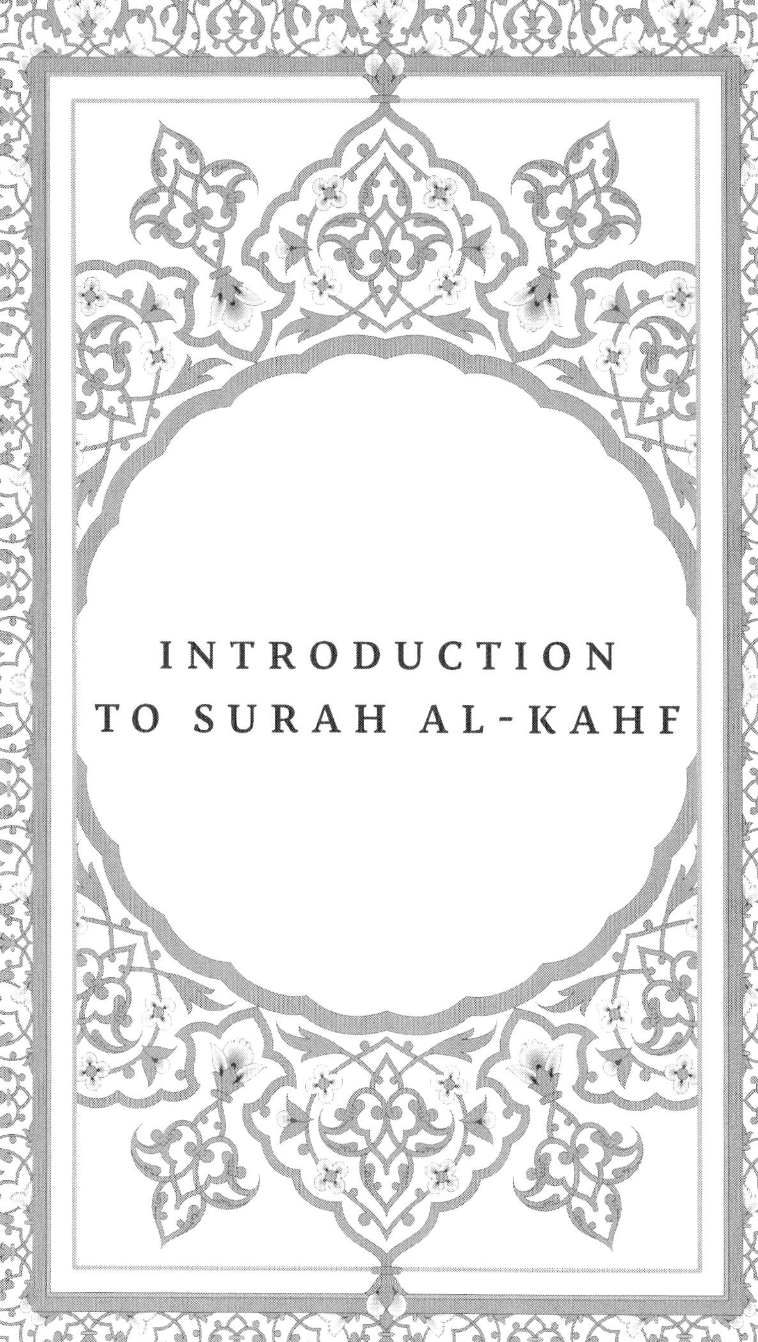

INTRODUCTION TO SURAH AL-KAHF

Sūrah al-Kahf is classified as a Makkan sūrah, meaning it was revealed before the migration of the Prophet ﷺ from Makkah to Madinah, and it consists of 110 verses. It is considered to be a part of late Makkan revelation. The Quran was not revealed in a vacuum. In order to understand the message of a verse or sūrah, it is important to understand its context. The Prophet ﷺ spent a very difficult thirteen years in Makkah. People who knew him as the most honest and trustworthy now called him a liar, a forger, a sorcerer, a magician, and even a mad man. He was seen as a direct threat to the status quo. The people who initially accepted Islam were generally weak and poor, and faced persecution at the hands of the Quraysh. After migration, the Muslims gained strength, power, and influence. The issues they dealt with in Madinah were very different from the issues they dealt with in Makkah. That is one of the reasons why there is a noticeable difference in themes and subject matter of revelation before and after migration. It is named after the unique and interesting story of the People of the Cave discussed in verses 9-26, which serves as a clear proof of the might, power, glory, and magnificence of Allah ﷻ.

Just like most Makkan revelation, it deals primarily with issues related to īmān, faith and belief. Makkan revelation generally deals with three concepts in different ways and styles:

1. Affirming the Oneness of Allah (al-Tawḥīd),
2. Prophethood and Messengership (al-Risālah), and
3. Life After Death (al-Qiyāmah).

Syed Quṭb ﵀ mentions that the central theme of the Sūrah is to purge faith of all alien concepts. "It seeks to establish correct and accurate thought and reasoning in order to establish values that are sound according to the criterion of Islam... It is to make faith the basis for the evaluation of concepts, ideas, practices and values."[10] That's part of the reason why the Sūrah starts and ends with declaring Allah's oneness and accepting revelation as the absolute truth.

The Sūrah is made up of four main stories:

1. The Companions of the Cave (v. 9-26),
2. The Owner of the Two Gardens (v. 32-44),
3. Mūsa ﵇ and al-Khaḍir (v. 60-82), and
4. Dhū al-Qarnayn (v. 83-101)

These four stories make up the majority of the Sūrah, taking up approximately 71 out of the 110 verses. In between these four narratives, we'll find various warnings to the non-believers and descriptions of the Day of Judgment.

VIRTUES OF SŪRAH AL-KAHF

One of the reasons for choosing to compile a short explanation of Sūrah al-Kahf is because there are several narrations in which we are encouraged to recite and memorize it.

عَن أَبِي الدَّرْدَاءِ ﵁ أَنَّ نَبِيَّ اللَّهِ ﷺ قَالَ "مَنْ حَفِظَ عَشْرَ آيَاتٍ مِنْ أَوَّلِ سُورَةِ الْكَهْفِ عُصِمَ مِنْ فِتْنَةِ الدَّجَّالِ" وَفِي رِوايَةٍ: "مِنْ آخِرِ سورةِ الْكَهْفِ"

In the ḥadīth collections of Muslim, Abū Dāwūd, al-Nasā'ī, and al-Tirmidhī we find a narration of Abū Dardā'a ﵁ in which he narrates that the

10 Quṭb, *fī Ẓilāl al-Quran*, 4:2257

Prophet ﷺ said, "Whoever memorizes the first ten verses of Sūrah al-Kahf will be protected from the Dajjāl[11]." In another narration it mentions the last ten verses.[12]

فَمَنْ أَدْرَكَهُ مِنْكُمْ فَلْيَقْرَأْ عَلَيْهِ فَوَاتِحَ سُورَةِ الْكَهْفِ

In a longer narration that talks about Dajjāl and the trials that come along with him, the Prophet ﷺ told us to recite the beginning of Sūrah al-Kahf for protection against him.[13]

عَن أَنَس ﷺ أَنَّهُ قَالَ: مَن قَرَأَ بِهَا أُعطِيَ نُورًا بَينَ السَّمَاءِ وَالأَرضِ وَوُقِيَ بِهَا فِتنَةَ القَبر

In another narration it is mentioned that whoever reads it will be given light between heaven and earth and it will protect him from the trial of the grave.[14]

"مَن قَرَأَ الكَهفَ يَومَ الجُمُعَةِ أَضَاءَ لَهُ مِنَ النُّورِ مَا بَينَ الجُمُعَتَينِ"

Abū Saīd al-Khudrī ﷺ narrates that the Prophet ﷺ said, "Whoever recites al-Kahf on Friday, a light will be illuminated for him until the following Friday."[15]

---

11 al-Dajjāl is the Antichrist or the False Messiah. He is a false prophet that will emerge near the end of times and his emergence is considered to be one of the major signs of the Last Day. He will spread corruption and disbelief throughout the world primarily through material exploitation by claiming divinity leading many people astray. Devout believers will be able to recognize him by the word "non-believer" written on his forehead. He will emerge shortly before the second coming of Isa ﷺ who will serve as the leader of the Muslims who will eventually defeat al-Dajjāl.

12 Muslim, *k. ṣalāh al-musāfirīn wa qaṣrihā, b. faḍl sūrah al-kahf wa ayah al-kursī*, 809

13 Muslim, *k. al-fitan wa ashrāṭ al-sāʿah, b. dhikr al-dajjāl wa ṣifatuhu wa mā maʿahu*, 2937

14 Qurṭubī, *al-Jāmiʿ li Aḥkām al-Quran*, 13:197

15 Suyūṭī, *al-Jāmiʿ al-Ṣaghīr*, 8910

"مَـن قَرَأَهَـا لَيلَـةَ الجُمُعَـةِ أَضَـاءَ لَهُ مِـنَ النُّـورِ مَـا بَينَـهُ وَبَـينَ البَيـتِ العَتِيق"

Another version of the same ḥadīth mentions that a light will be illuminated between them and the "Ancient House," meaning the Kabah.[16]

From ibn Isḥāq who said: "I heard al-Barā' ﷺ saying that a man recited al-Kahf while there was an animal nearby that became startled. He looked and found a cloud shadowing it. He mentioned that to the Prophet ﷺ who said, '[Continue] reciting because that is tranquility (sakīnah) that descends during recitation of the Quran.'" [17]

Imām al-Qurṭubī ﷺ in his famous Tafsīr narrates a report that mentions whoever recites the last five verses of Sūrah al-Kahf before going to sleep, then Allah ﷻ will wake them up at any time in the night they want.[18] One of the narrators of this report mentions that he tried it and it worked. Meaning, it serves as some sort of spiritual alarm clock.

CONNECTION BETWEEN SŪRAH AL-KAHF AND THE DAJJĀL

After reading some of these narrations, a few questions that naturally arise are, "What is the connection between this noble Sūrah and the Dajjāl?" "How will reciting Sūrah al-Kahf protect me from the trials of Dajjāl?" When we reflect upon Sūrah al-Kahf, we will find that its message conveys certain ideas and tools that are extremely beneficial in protecting us from the trials of this world and the Dajjāl. Sūrah al-Kahf discusses four stories that are representative of four different types of trials (fitan) and four causes of salvation from those trials:

---

16 Dhahabī, *al-Muhadhdhab*, 3:1181

17 Muslim, *k. ṣalāh al-musāfirīn wa qaṣrihā, b. nuzūl al-sakīnah lī qirā'ah al-quran*, 795

18 Dāramī, *Musnad*, 2409

1.

The first story is about the Companions of the Cave (Aṣḥāb al-Kahf), which represents the fitnah (trial) of faith. It highlights how a group of young men were tested because of their faith and what they had to do in order to protect it.

This is a story about a group of young men who remained firm, steadfast, and patient upon their faith in the face of hardship, difficulty, and threat of persecution. They were living in a society of disbelief and immorality and decided to seek refuge in a cave to protect their own faith. Allah ﷻ miraculously protected them and when they awoke they found that their entire community had become believers.

Their protection from this challenge and way of overcoming it was their concern for their spiritual well-being, their īmān, and righteous companionship.

2.

The second story is regarding the owner of two gardens, which represents the fitnah of wealth and children. It highlights how the love of this world and material possessions can corrupt a person's heart and blind them from seeing the truth.

This is a story about an extremely wealthy man whom Allah ﷻ had blessed with wealth, property, and children. Instead of being grateful and thankful, he became extremely arrogant and prideful. His friend reminded him that all of his blessings were gifts from Allah ﷻ, but he refused to acknowledge the truth and was blinded by material means. As a result, Allah ﷻ afflicted him with difficulties by taking away his wealth.

Protection from this type of trial lies in gratitude and recognizing the reality of the life of this world; recognizing that the life of this world is temporary and fleeting and that the life of the world to come is everlasting.

3.

The third story is about Mūsa ﷺ and al-Khaḍir, which represents the trial of knowledge. It highlights the importance of continuously seeking knowledge and humbling oneself while doing so with patience.

Mūsa ﷺ was asked about the most knowledgeable person on the face of the Earth. Since he was unaware of anyone more knowledgeable than himself, he answered that he was. Allah ﷻ then revealed to him that there was someone more knowledgeable than him and Mūsa ﷺ then traveled in search of him. After finding him, he spent some time in his company and saw him doing things that he couldn't understand because they seemingly contradicted God's law that was revealed to him. The key to dealing with this trial is through humility and patience.

4.

The fourth story is about a powerful and just ruler who is mentioned as Dhū al-Qarnayn. It is an example of how a person successfully dealt with the trial of power, leadership, and authority.

This is the story of a great ruler who was given both knowledge and power and traveled the earth relieving hardship and spreading goodness. He solved the problem of Yajūj and Majūj[19] by sealing them in the earth and in doing so was able to mobilize the resources of a people who could hardly understand his speech. We learn that he was able to protect himself from the corruptive nature of power and authority through sincerity and service.

The four trials or temptations highlighted in these narratives are part of the trials and tribulations that will be brought by the Dajjāl. He will travel across the world performing seemingly supernatural acts, claiming divinity. He will tell people to follow and worship him, which will be a test of people's faith. We learn from this Sūrah that one of the most effective ways of safeguarding our īmān is through genuine concern and good company. Allah ﷻ tells us in verse 28, "And keep yourself content with those who call their Lord morning and evening, seeking His pleasure, and let not your eyes overlook them, seeking the splendor of the worldly life. And do not obey the one whose heart We have made heedless of Our remembrance, and who has followed his desire and whose behavior has exceeded the limits."

Dajjāl will test people by enticing them through wealth and material possessions. He will command the sky to send down rain and will seduce and deceive people due to the amount of wealth he will possess. In Sūrah al-Kahf, we learn that one of the best ways to protect ourselves from the love of this world and material wealth is through recognizing the reality of the life of this

---

19 A group of people that will be described later in the book.

world. Allah ﷻ says in verse 45, "And give them a parable of this worldly life. [It is] like the plants of the earth, thriving when sustained by the rain We send down from the sky. Then they [soon] turn into chaff scattered by the wind. And Allah is fully capable of [doing] all things."

He will be a trial for people through the information he will possess and relay. People will be tricked, deceived, and fooled by his level of knowledge and intelligence. From the narrative of Mūsa ﵇ and al-Khaḍir, we learn that one of the ways of protecting ourselves from that is intellectual humility and patience.

When the Dajjāl emerges he will be some sort of a "world leader." He will have control over many parts of the world. Obviously, he will be corrupt and not care to be just. However, we learn from the story of Dhū al-Qarnayn that one of the ways of protecting ourselves from the corrupting nature of power and leadership is through sincerity and a genuine desire to serve and help others.

I'm sure there are several other connections that can be derived between the message of Sūrah al-Kahf and the trials of Dajjāl. A good exercise would be to study the Sūrah deeply and try to extract those connections. It is important to understand that these are connections that we understand and they may or may not be correct. What we do know is that the Prophet ﷺ taught us to recite the first or last ten verses of Sūrah al-Kahf as a means of protecting ourselves from the trials of Dajjāl. May Allah ﷻ protect all of us from the fitnah of the Dajjāl and all other fitan, both apparent and hidden.

CAUSE OF REVELATION

Regarding the background in which this Sūrah was revealed, Imām al-Qurṭubī ﵀ narrates a report from ibn Isḥāq that mentions that the Quraysh sent two men, al-Naḍr ibn al-Ḥārtih and Uqbah ibn abī Muayṭ, to the Jewish scholars of Madinah to ask them about the Prophet ﷺ. The Quraysh told these two men to ask the Rabbis about Muḥammad ﷺ, his characteristics, qualities, and to inform them about some of his teachings because they knew more about Prophets since they were People of the Book. They arrived in Madinah and told the Rabbis about Muḥammad ﷺ; his characteristics, qualities, description, message, and teachings.

The Rabbis told them to go back and ask the Prophet ﷺ three questions; if he answers them correctly then he is a Prophet and a Messenger and if he doesn't answer them then he is an imposter. Ask him about the young men who left their city in the distant past and what happened to them, because this is a unique event. Ask him about the person who traveled the East and the West and what happened to him. Ask him about the soul and what it is. If he answers these three questions, follow him because he is a Prophet. If he doesn't, then he's an imposter and you can do as you please with his message.

They came back excitedly and shared their conversation with the leadership of Quraysh. They came to the Prophet ﷺ and posed these three questions to him. The Prophet ﷺ told them that he would reply to them the next day expecting Allah ﷻ to send down revelation, but he forgot to say "if Allah wills." Allah ﷻ didn't send down any revelation for the next fifteen days, and according to another narration it was only three days. Because of the slight delay, the Quraysh began to assume that he didn't know the answers and that his claims to prophethood were false. After fifteen days (or three) Allah ﷻ revealed the entire Sūrah and reminded the Prophet ﷺ to always say in shā'a Allah.[20]

20 Qurṭubī, *al-Jāmiʿ li Aḥkām al-Quran*, 13: 198-199

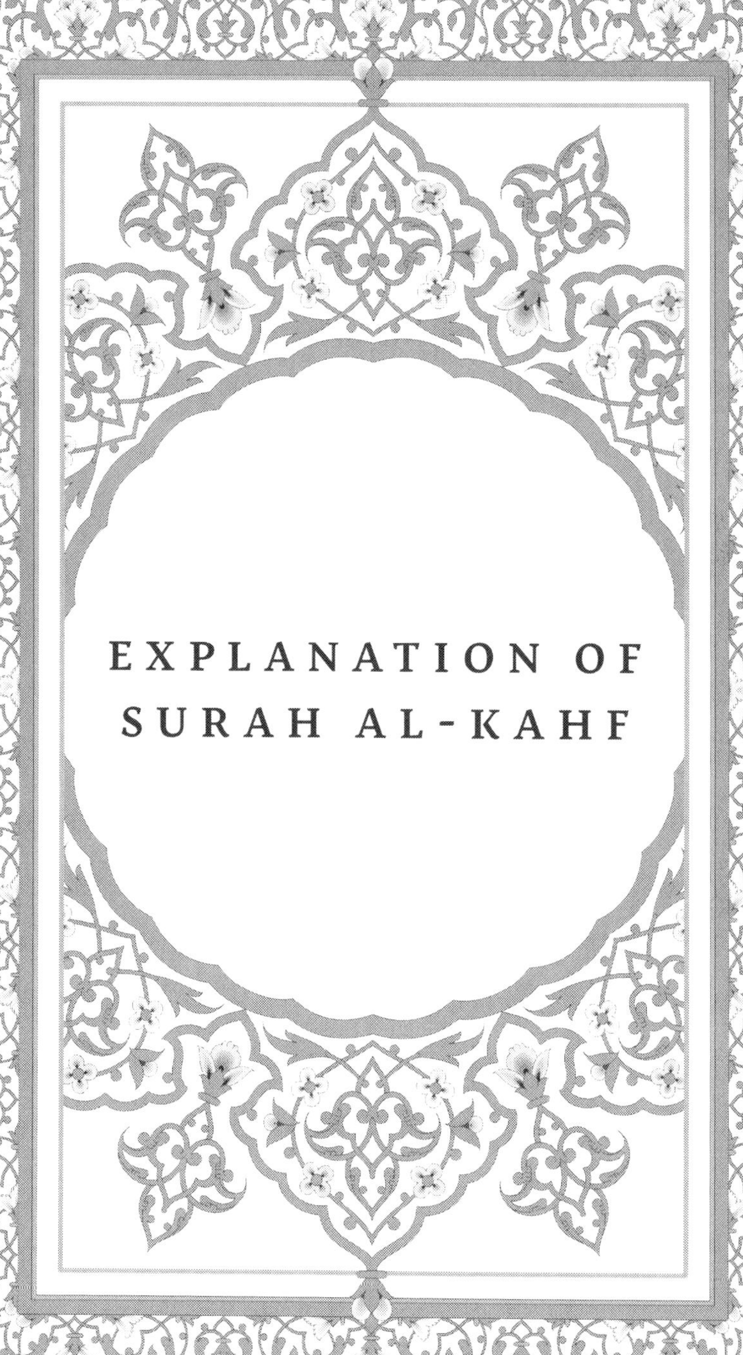

EXPLANATION OF SURAH AL-KAHF

VERSES 1-3

الْحَمْدُ لِلَّهِ الَّذِى أَنزَلَ عَلَىٰ عَبْدِهِ الْكِتَابَ وَلَمْ يَجْعَل لَّهُ عِوَجَا ۜ
﴿١﴾ قَيِّمًا لِّيُنذِرَ بَأْسًا شَدِيدًا مِّن لَّدُنْهُ وَيُبَشِّرَ الْمُؤْمِنِينَ الَّذِينَ
يَعْمَلُونَ الصَّالِحَاتِ أَنَّ لَهُمْ أَجْرًا حَسَنًا ﴿٢﴾ مَّاكِثِينَ فِيهِ أَبَدًا ﴿٣﴾

[1] All praise is for Allah, Who sent down the Book to His servant, and allowed no crookedness in it, [2] perfectly upright, so that he may warn of a severe punishment from His Presence and give glad tidings to the believers who perform righteous deeds that they will have an excellent reward, [3] in which they will remain forever,

Allah ﷻ starts the Sūrah in a very beautiful, elegant, and eloquent way by teaching us how to be grateful for the infinite blessings He has favored us with; and more specifically how to express gratitude for the Quran, one of Allah's greatest gifts to humanity. The opening verses of the Sūrah deal with the concept of praise and gratitude and give us a brief description of the Quran.

The first verse starts with the words "al-ḥamd lillāh", which is usually translated as "Praise belongs to Allah," "All praise is for Allah," or "All praise and thanks are due to Allah." It is one of five Sūrahs in the Quran that start with these words. The others are al-Fātiḥah, al-Anām, Saba', and Fāṭir. The word al-ḥamd is translated as praise; however its meaning is much more comprehensive than simply praise. It denotes praising someone with goodness for what they have done consciously as a favor or because of some inherent quality. Several scholars define it as verbal praise for something that is done voluntarily, regardless of whether it is a favor or not[21]. [22] Ḥamd is praise along with acknowledgment of noteworthy qualities and actions done out of genuine love, veneration, reverence, gratitude, and appreciation. It includes extolling Allah ﷻ, praising Him, and giving thanks to Him for all of the favors and blessings He has given us in this world and for the reward that He will give us in the next.

The word ḥamd has sister terms in Arabic that are very close and similar in meaning such as madḥ and shukr. Madḥ is general praise; when you praise someone or something for noteworthy qualities or actions that are voluntary or involuntary.[23] In English, we can think of madḥ more as a compliment. For example, we might compliment someone on their looks, intelligence, or eloquence. Shukr is gratitude; it's always done as a response to a favor that someone has done for us and can be expressed through the heart, tongue, or limbs. Through this lens, the word ḥamd is much more comprehensive than both madḥ and shukr; madḥ is too wide in scope and shukr is too narrow because it's only done in response to a favor.

Another way of looking at it is that ḥamd is praise coupled with gratitude done out of genuine love, reverence, and appreciation. It includes praising Allah ﷻ and giving thanks to Him for all of the innumerable favors and

---

21 الحَمدُ هُوَ الثَّنَاءُ بِاللِّسَانِ عَلَى الجَمِيلِ الاِختِيَارِيِّ مِن نِعمَةٍ وَغَيرِهَا

22 Qārī, *Mirqāt al-Mafātīḥ*, 1:48

23 المَدحُ هُوَ الثَّنَاءُ بِاللِّسَانِ عَلَى الجَمِيلِ الاِختِيَارِيِّ وَغَيرِ الاِختِيَارِيِّ

blessings He has given to us. Ibn Abbās ﵄ said, "al-Ḥamd lillāh is the statement of every thankful servant."[24] This is the phrase that Allah ﷻ has taught human beings to use in order to praise Him. Every single blessing a person enjoys in this world is directly from Allah ﷻ. "And every blessing you have is from Allah."[25] Allah ﷻ is constantly showering us with His blessings, favors, and mercy. The reality is that Allah ﷻ has blessed us with an innumerable amount of gifts and blessings; they can't be quantified. As Allah ﷻ Himself tell us in the Quran, "And if you were to count the blessings of Allah, you would not be able to quantify them. Truly mankind is unjust, ungrateful."[26] Just take our bodies for example. In our eyes and our ability to see, our noses and ability to smell, our ears and ability to hear, our hands and feet and ability to feel, in every joint, every bone, every muscle, every organ, every vein, and every cell are countless blessings. Not only are we unable to count all of these blessings or even imagine them, we're also unable to properly thank Allah ﷻ for them.

By starting with al-ḥamd lillāh, Allah ﷻ is teaching us the best words to use to thank Him and express gratitude to Him. The Prophet ﷺ said, "When you say, 'Praise be to God, Lord of the worlds,' you will have thanked God and He will increase your bounty."[27] Similarly, the Prophet ﷺ when supplicating used to say, "There is no way to enumerate the praise due to You; You are as You have praised Yourself."[28] Allah ﷻ is also reminding us that all praise and thanks exclusively belong to Him ﷻ. That's why the word "ḥamd" is definite. Even the definite particle "al" in the Arabic Language carries meaning. One of the meanings it carries is that of istighrāq, or comprehensiveness. Literally every and all types of praise are for Allah ﷻ. Whenever we praise anything in this world we are ultimately praising Allah ﷻ because He is the source of every single thing that exists. The world is made of millions of things that attract our attention and admiration, and if we move beyond what we see physically or materially, we will find in each and every single thing a manifestation of the greatness of Allah ﷻ. All Praise is exclusively for Allah ﷻ because He is the one that is showering us with blessings at every single mo-

---

24 Qurṭubī, *al-Jāmiʿ li Aḥkām al-Quran*, 1:133

25 16:53 وَمَا بِكُم مِّن نِّعْمَةٍ فَمِنَ اللَّـهِ

26 14:34 وَإِن تَعُدُّوا نِعْمَتَ اللَّـهِ لَا تُحْصُوهَا ۗ إِنَّ الْإِنسَانَ لَظَلُومٌ كَفَّارٌ

27 Ṭabarī, *Tafsīr al-Ṭabarī*, 1:136

28 Bayhaqī, *Shuʿab al-Īmān*, 3837

ment of our lives. Allah ﷻ praises Himself at the beginning and end of all affairs because He is the One who is constantly being praised.

Allah ﷻ then tells us one of the infinite reasons why we praise Him. "Who sent down the Book to His servant, and allowed no crookedness in it, (2) perfectly upright."

"His servant" is referring to the Messenger of Allah, our master and beloved, Muhammad ﷺ. The title "abd (servant)" is the highest spiritual station we can reach as human beings. In this context abd is an honorific title, a title of high rank and status, a title of love and endearment. When attributed to the Prophet ﷺ, it's an honorific title. al-Kitāb, literally the Book, is one of the titles of the Quran. It can mean that which is read as well as that which is written. One of the reasons why it has been called al-Kitāb is because the Quran is preserved both orally and through writing.

Here, Allah ﷻ is reminding us of one of the greatest gifts given to humanity; the Quran. That He alone is the One who has revealed the Book to Muhammad ﷺ as a source of guidance for all of humanity until the end of time. It is one of the greatest blessings because it is a roadmap towards success; towards a life that is pleasing to the Divine. Through the guidance of this book, Allah ﷻ removed mankind from the darkness of ignorance and disbelief to the light of knowledge and belief. It teaches us how to be successful in the life of this world and more importantly in the life of the world to come. The Quran is the absolute most important book in our lives because the Quran isn't simply a book; it is the divine speech of Allah ﷻ -- His words revealed to the Prophet ﷺ. It is our primary source of beliefs, rituals, ethics, morals, principles, laws, and guidance. Our entire lives as Muslims are supposed to revolve around the teachings of the Quran. It is our source of guidance to navigate through the world and live a life that is pleasing to Allah ﷻ. It is literally our manual for life that we use to build a path towards the Divine. It is our source of inspiration, encouragement, and the tool we use to deal with the different challenges of life. It contains guidance for every single aspect of our lives.

Allah ﷻ then provides two descriptions of the Quran. The first is, "and allowed no crookedness in it..." There's absolutely no crookedness in the Quran, which means that the Quran isn't confusing or difficult to understand. There are no contradictions in it in terms of words or meanings. It is free from all kinds of excess and deficiencies. The Quran is balanced and harmonious. When something is crooked, it's difficult to follow. The Quran is straight and easy to follow. As Allah ﷻ tells us in Sūrah al-Qamar, "And indeed We have made the Quran easy to remember; so is there anyone who remembers?"[29] One of the reasons for mentioning this here is to refute the false claims of the people of Makkah that the Quran is poetry, magic, ancient tales, or a human composition. All of these are man-made and can be full of contradictions and mistakes.

The second description of the Quran is that it is "perfectly upright." Meaning, the Quran is straightforward, perfect in words and meaning, guiding towards the straight path. The Quran can't be corrupted; it can't be altered or changed in any way shape or form. It is under the divine protection of Allah ﷻ. As Allah ﷻ tells us in Sūrah Fussilat, "Falsehood comes not upon it from before it or from behind it; a revelation from the All-Wise, Praised."[30] The word "qayyim" or upright is used elsewhere in the Quran to describe Islam itself. But here it's being used to describe the Quran, which emphasizes that there's no crookedness in it. The word "qayyim" can also mean a guard or custodian. So the meaning would then be that the Quran is a custodian of all previously revealed scriptures, confirming what's in them and a witness to their truth. It can also mean that the Quran takes care of the needs of humanity highlighting those things that are beneficial and preventing those things that are harmful.

Allah ﷻ then tells us about two main reasons or objectives behind the revelation of the Quran. "... So that he may warn of a severe punishment from His Presence and give glad tidings to the believers who perform righteous deeds that they will have an excellent reward, in which they will remain forever." Among the objectives of revelation is to warn the disbelievers and give glad tidings to the believers. Through the Quran, Allah ﷻ warns those who choose to disbelieve about a severe punishment from Allah ﷻ, both in this world and the next. Allah ﷻ also gives good news or glad tidings to the believers, those who believe in the Quran and affirm their faith with righteous deeds, that for them is a good reward, which is Paradise. They will live in Paradise forever.

This brings up a very important point; īmān is something that is active and alive. It translates into action expressing itself through our speech,

---

29 54:17 وَلَقَدْ يَسَّرْنَا الْقُرْآنَ لِلذِّكْرِ فَهَلْ مِن مُّدَّكِرٍ

30 41:42 لَّا يَأْتِيهِ الْبَاطِلُ مِن بَيْنِ يَدَيْهِ وَلَا مِنْ خَلْفِهِ ۖ تَنزِيلٌ مِّنْ حَكِيمٍ حَمِيدٍ

behavior, choices, and deeds. Īmān is always paired with righteous deeds throughout the Quran. It is this combination of īmān and righteous deeds that leads towards Paradise.

Warning and giving glad tidings was the responsibility of every single Prophet and Messenger that was sent to humanity. To warn humanity about the dangers and consequences of disbelief and to give humanity the glad tidings of forgiveness, grace, mercy, reward, and paradise for those who believe. Allah ﷻ tells us, "Mankind was one community; then Allah sent the prophets as bearers of glad tidings and as warners."[31] Allah ﷻ tells us about the Prophet ﷺ, "O Prophet! Truly We have sent you as a witness, as a bearer of glad tidings and as a warner, as one who calls unto God by His leave and as a luminous lamp." [32]

Allah ﷻ then makes the warning specific to a certain group of disbelievers, those who said that Allah ﷻ has a child.

VERSES 4-5

وَيُنذِرَ الَّذِينَ قَالُوا اتَّخَذَ اللَّهُ وَلَدًا ﴿٤﴾ مَّا لَهُم بِهِ مِنْ عِلْمٍ وَلَا
لِآبَائِهِمْ ۚ كَبُرَتْ كَلِمَةً تَخْرُجُ مِنْ أَفْوَاهِهِمْ ۚ إِن يَقُولُونَ إِلَّا كَذِبًا ﴿٥﴾

4 and so that He may warn those who say, "God has taken a child." 5 They have no knowledge of this, nor do their forefathers. A monstrous word it is that issues from their mouths. They say nothing but a lie.

---

31 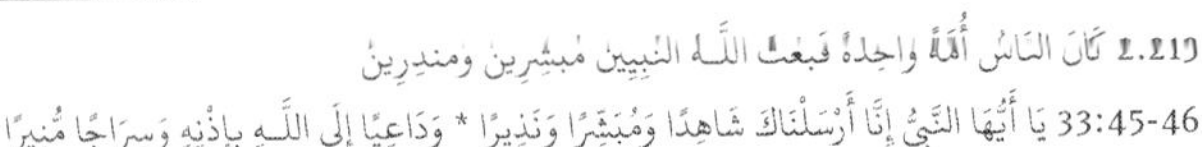
2:213 كَانَ النَّاسُ أُمَّةً وَاحِدَةً فَبَعَثَ اللَّهُ النَّبِيِّينَ مُبَشِّرِينَ وَمُنذِرِينَ

32 33:45-46 يَا أَيُّهَا النَّبِيُّ إِنَّا أَرْسَلْنَاكَ شَاهِدًا وَمُبَشِّرًا وَنَذِيرًا * وَدَاعِيًا إِلَى اللَّهِ بِإِذْنِهِ وَسِرَاجًا مُّنِيرًا

Verse number four is referring to three specific groups of people:

1. Polytheists of Makkah
2. Jews
3. Christians

The Mushrikūn (Polytheists) of Makkah believed that Angels were the daughters of Allah ﷻ. The Christians claimed that Īsā ﷺ was the son of God and some Jews claimed that Uzair ﷺ was the son of God. The reason why Allah ﷻ specifies these three groups is to show that this is the worst type of disbelief. It is considered to be one of the worst types of disbelief because there is no evidence for it whatsoever; it's based on pure ignorance. "They have no knowledge thereof, nor do their forefathers." Basically, they're blindly following the religion, customs, and traditions of their forefathers without questioning them whatsoever. They're not using their minds and thinking on their own.

Throughout the Quran, Allah ﷻ encourages us to use our intellect to recognize the truth. Blindly following one's parents, grandparents, forefathers, and customs in terms of religious beliefs and practices has been looked down upon. In addition to that, to ascribe a child to Allah ﷻ is blasphemous; it's a huge claim to make without any proof. "A monstrous word it is that issues from their mouths. They say nothing but a lie." To say something like that is a big deal; it carries a lot of weight and sin. It's literally a monstrosity that's coming out of their mouths and it's an absolute lie that has no reality to it whatsoever. Allah ﷻ says in Sūrah Maryam, "It almost causes the heavens to be torn apart, the earth to split asunder, the mountains to crumble to pieces, that they attribute offspring to the Lord of Mercy."[33] This concept of God having a child has been categorically rejected in several places throughout the Quran. This claim of theirs is a fabrication upon Allah ﷻ.

The Sūrah now turns to console and comfort the Prophet ﷺ telling him not to worry and be so sad about the continual disbelief of his people. This is an extremely beautiful aspect of the Quran. The Lord of the worlds consoles and comforts the last and final Messenger through revelation. The Prophet ﷺ had extreme concern and care for his people; he wanted every single person to achieve eternal salvation. The Makkan period of Prophethood was

33 19:90-91 تَكَادُ السَّمَاوَاتُ يَتَفَطَّرْنَ مِنْهُ وَتَنشَقُّ الْأَرْضُ وَتَخِرُّ الْجِبَالُ هَدًّا * أَن دَعَوْا لِلرَّحْمَٰنِ وَلَدًا

full of difficulty and hardships. The Prophet ﷺ was mocked, ridiculed, harassed, and abused both verbally and physically. His Companions faced verbal and physical persecution. These difficulties definitely had an effect on the psyche, morale, and emotions of both the Prophet and His companions. The Prophet ﷺ would feel concern, grief, sorrow and sadness at the fact that his own people are rejecting him and his message. Throughout Makkan revelation we find Allah ﷻ consoling, comforting, and reassuring the Prophet ﷺ; reminding him to be strong, patient, steadfast, not to worry about the reaction of his people, and to place his trust fully in Allah ﷻ.

فَلَعَلَّكَ بَاخِعٌ نَّفْسَكَ عَلَىٰ آثَارِهِمْ إِن لَّمْ يُؤْمِنُوا بِهَٰذَا الْحَدِيثِ
أَسَفًا ٦

[6] Perhaps you would destroy yourself with grief for their sake, if they don't believe in this account.

Allah ﷻ is comforting, consoling, and reassuring the Prophet ﷺ; don't be so sad, distraught, and depressed at their refusal to believe in the Quran. Don't grieve out of sorrow for them if they refuse to accept the message. "This account" is referring to the Quran. "Destroy yourself with grief" is understood to mean "to expend yourself in grief and sorrow"[34]. Your responsibility is simply to convey the message; you are not responsible for what they do with it. Once they have received the message, they are responsible for their own decisions. If they accept the truth, then

34 Rāzī, *al-Tafsīr al-Kabīr*, 21:426

they will be benefiting themselves and if they reject it, then they will only be harming themselves. Allah ﷻ consoles and comforts the Prophet ﷺ with similar remarks in Sūrah Fāṭir saying, "God leaves whoever He wills to stray and guides whoever He wills. [Prophet], do not waste your soul away with regret for them: God knows exactly what they do."[35] Allah ﷻ also says in Sūrah al-Shuarā', "Perhaps you [O Prophet] will grieve yourself to death over their disbelief."[36]

The Sūrah then reminds the readers and listeners about the reality of the life of this world. Allah ﷻ informs us about the mortal and fleeting nature of this world; that this world is a place of tests and trials and that it is not permanent.

VERSES 7-8

إِنَّا جَعَلْنَا مَا عَلَى الْأَرْضِ زِينَةً لَّهَا لِنَبْلُوَهُمْ أَيُّهُمْ أَحْسَنُ عَمَلًا ۝٧
وَإِنَّا لَجَاعِلُونَ مَا عَلَيْهَا صَعِيدًا جُرُزًا ۝٨

[7] We have indeed made whatever is on earth an adornment for it, in order to test which of them is best in deeds. [8] And We will certainly reduce whatever is on it to barren ground.

In verse seven, Allah ﷻ is telling us that every single thing on this Earth is a type of adornment or beautification; it's meant to attract us and distract us as a test and trial. That's the purpose of adornment and beautification (zīnah); to attract and draw a person's attention towards it. The adorn-

35 35:8

36 26:3

ment of this world pulls us towards it creating a very powerful distraction for us as human beings from our true purpose in life. The dunyā - material wealth and possessions, enjoyments and pleasures - is a test for us as human beings. Allah ﷻ Himself tells us that one of the objectives behind this test is to see "which of them is best in deeds." How are we, as human beings, going to respond to this test? Will we be distracted and get caught up in the life of this world? Or will we be grateful and thankful to Allah ﷻ for all of His countless blessings? Will the adornment and allure of this world take a person away from their purpose in life or will they remain firm and steadfast upon their faith? Ubayy ؓ would say, "Most virtuous in deed means to take [from this world] rightfully, to spend rightfully with belief, fulfill obligations, stay away from prohibitions, and perform a lot of recommended deeds."[37] Imām al-Qurṭubī ؒ also mentions that the Prophet ﷺ captured the essence of what this means when he said, "Say I believe in Allah and then remain steadfast."[38]

The idea of the dunyā as a distraction and test is something that has been mentioned throughout the Quran. In several places, Allah ﷻ reminds us to not be fooled and deceived by the pleasures and enjoyments of this world. Similarly the Prophet ﷺ told us, "This world is sweet and green, and Allah makes you generations coming one after the other, so He is watching what you will do. Beware of (the beguilements of) this world and beware of women, for the first affliction that the Children of Israel suffered from was that of women."[39]

In the next verse, Allah ﷻ reminds us that this world is temporary and will eventually come to an end. "And We will certainly reduce whatever is on it to barren ground." Every single thing we see around us; every single human being, animal, insect, plant, fruit, vegetable, tree, whatever you can think of has a limited life span. Every single thing in this world will cease to exist. Everything has a time limit or an expiration date. The Heavens and the Earth and everything they contain - the planets, stars, galaxies, celestial bodies, mountains, rivers, oceans, this entire universe - will cease to exist. The universe will be made non-existent and the only being remaining will be

37 Qurṭubī, *al-Jāmiʿ li Aḥkām al-Quran*, 13:209

38 Muslim, *k. al-īmān*, *b. jāmiʿ awṣāf al-islām*, 38

39 Muslim, *k. al-riqāq*, *b. akthar ahl al-jannah al-fuqarāʾa wa akthat ahl al-nār al-nisāʾa*, 2742

Allah ﷻ the Almighty, the All-Powerful, the Ever-Living, the Ever-Lasting, the Eternal. As Allah ﷻ tells us in Sūrah al-Raḥmān, "Everyone on Earth perishes; All that remains is the Face of your Lord, full of majesty, bestowing honor."[40] Similarly Allah ﷻ tells us in Sūrah al-Qaṣaṣ, "Everything is bound to perish except He Himself. All authority belongs to Him. And to Him you will [all] be returned."[41]

One of the most powerful and constant reminders throughout the Quran is that the life of this world is temporary; that you and I, we're not going to be here forever. And that the life to come, the life of the Hereafter, is a life of eternity. There are so many things that we work for and invest in throughout our lives. We run after them, but in the end what happens? All of it ceases to exist. It no longer matters. The only thing that actually remains is the consequences of our faith.

Now, Allah ﷻ turns our attention to the story of the People of the Cave, from which the Sūrah gets its name. As mentioned in the introduction to the Sūrah, this account was revealed to the Prophet ﷺ in response to three specific questions posed by the leadership of Quraysh. This is an extremely famous story that is also related in the Biblical tradition. There it is referred to as the story of the "Seven Sleepers of Ephesus."

Whenever a story is mentioned in the Quran, it is mentioned for a reason or purpose. One of those reasons is so that we can learn and extract lessons, morals, and reminders from it. The stories of the Quran are not entertainment or simple historical facts. Rather, they are there so that we can study them and derive lessons, morals, and reminders that we can use in our daily lives. That is one of the reasons why we find that Allah ﷻ has not related a complete story in chronological order, from beginning to end, with all its details.The only exception to this, and it's a partial exception, is the narrative of Yūsuf ﷺ mentioned in Sūrah Yūsuf. He ﷻ only relates those parts of the story that are relevant and related to guidance. As Allah ﷻ says, "Surely, in the narratives of these, there is a lesson for the people of understanding. It is not an invented story, rather, a confirmation of what has been before it, and an elaboration of everything, and guidance and mercy for a people who be-

---

40 55:26-27 كُلُّ مَنْ عَلَيْهَا فَانٍ * وَيَبْقَىٰ وَجْهُ رَبِّكَ ذُو الْجَلَالِ وَالْإِكْرَامِ

41 28:88 كُلُّ شَيْءٍ هَالِكٌ إِلَّا وَجْهَهُ ۚ لَهُ الْحُكْمُ وَإِلَيْهِ تُرْجَعُونَ

lieve."[42] For example, one of the objectives of this story is to serve as proof of Allah's power of resurrection and a reminder of the importance of safeguarding and protecting one's faith. In Sūrah Hūd, Allah ﷻ tells us, "We narrate to you all such stories from the events of the Messengers as We strengthen your heart therewith. And in these (stories) there has come to you the truth, a good counsel and a reminder to those who believe."[43] So another purpose of these stories is to also console, comfort, support, and provide strength to the Prophet ﷺ and his followers. Just as Allah ﷻ saved this very small group of believers from religious persecution, Allah ﷻ will also save and protect the Prophet ﷺ and his Companions.

This same method of relating stories is used in narrating this story; only the parts that are related to guidance have been mentioned. There is no mention of the remaining parts of the story that are purely historical or geographical. However, the commentators of the Quran, by studying historical and religious sources, have been able to provide these details. There are countless reports that speak about the sleepers in the cave, and just as many versions of their story. Their account is found in at least nine medieval languages and preserved in over 200 manuscripts, mainly dating to between the 9th and 13th centuries.[44] I will stick to the narrative as it is mentioned in the Tafsīr of ibn Kathīr.[45]

The Sūrah first introduces the story with a short summary before relating it in detail. This is a method that is employed elsewhere in the Quran as well. It grabs the attention of the listener and reciter.

---

42 12:111 لَقَدْ كَانَ فِي قَصَصِهِمْ عِبْرَةٌ لِأُولِي الْأَلْبَابِ ۗ مَا كَانَ حَدِيثًا يُفْتَرَىٰ وَلَٰكِن تَصْدِيقَ الَّذِي بَيْنَ يَدَيْهِ وَتَفْصِيلَ كُلِّ شَيْءٍ وَهُدًى وَرَحْمَةً لِّقَوْمٍ يُؤْمِنُونَ

43 11:120 وَكُلًّا نَّقُصُّ عَلَيْكَ مِنْ أَنبَاءِ الرُّسُلِ مَا نُثَبِّتُ بِهِ فُؤَادَكَ ۚ وَجَاءَكَ فِي هَٰذِهِ الْحَقُّ وَمَوْعِظَةٌ وَذِكْرَىٰ لِلْمُؤْمِنِينَ

44 Bartłomiej Grysa, "The Legend of the Seven Sleepers of Ephesus in Syriac and Arab Sources: A Comparative Study", Orientalia Christiana Cracoviensia 2 (2010): 45–59.

45 ibn Kathīr, *Tafsīr al-Quran al-ʿAẓīm*, 9:110

VERSES 9-12

أَمْ حَسِبْتَ أَنَّ أَصْحَابَ الْكَهْفِ وَالرَّقِيمِ كَانُوا مِنْ آيَاتِنَا عَجَبًا ﴿٩﴾
إِذْ أَوَى الْفِتْيَةُ إِلَى الْكَهْفِ فَقَالُوا رَبَّنَا آتِنَا مِن لَّدُنكَ رَحْمَةً وَهَيِّئْ
لَنَا مِنْ أَمْرِنَا رَشَدًا ﴿١٠﴾ فَضَرَبْنَا عَلَىٰ آذَانِهِمْ فِي الْكَهْفِ سِنِينَ عَدَدًا
﴿١١﴾ ثُمَّ بَعَثْنَاهُمْ لِنَعْلَمَ أَيُّ الْحِزْبَيْنِ أَحْصَىٰ لِمَا لَبِثُوا أَمَدًا ﴿١٢﴾

[9] Do you think that the people of the cave and the inscription were a wonder among Our signs? [10] When the youths took refuge in the cave, they said: 'Our Lord! Grant us mercy from Yourself, and provide us with right guidance in our affair.' [11] So We drew a veil over their ears in the cave, for a number of years, [12] and then We awakened them so that We could make clear which of the two parties was better able to calculate how long they had remained in that state.

These few verses summarize the entire incident of the Sleepers of Ephesus. Allah ﷻ introduces the story by asking the Prophet ﷺ a rhetorical question, "Do you think that the people of the cave and the inscription were a wonder among Our signs?" Even though this question is addressed directly to the Prophet ﷺ, it's actually directed towards the non-believers of Quraysh. Meaning, do you think that the story of the people of the cave and the inscription is something that is wondrous, amazing, miraculous, and extraordinary? If you do, then you should recognize that there are other "signs" that are even more wondrous in nature, such as the creation of the heavens and the earth and everything that they contain. The natural order of the world is itself a greater wonder and miracle than the occasional alteration of its regularity through miracles. There are many more things that are much more marvelous and miraculous in the universe than the story of the people of the cave.

In this verse, the seven sleepers are also referred to as the "people of the cave and the inscription." The inscription refers literally to an inscription that was made on a tablet that was placed at the entrance of the cave that detailed their story;[46] basically, a historical document that mentioned the details of who these individuals were and what happened to them.

Allah ﷻ then summarizes their story very briefly saying, "When the youths took refuge in the cave, they said: 'Our Lord! Grant us mercy from Yourself, and provide us with right guidance in our affair.' So We drew a veil over their ears in the cave, for a number of years, and then We awakened them so that We could make clear which of the two parties was better able to calculate how long they had remained in that state."

Meaning, remember or mention to your people when the youths took refuge in the cave for the sake of their religion, fleeing from religious persecution. When they entered the cave they turned to Allah ﷻ in supplication asking Him for His mercy, grace, guidance, and protection. In this supplication they asked specifically for two things:

1. Mercy, and
2. Right guidance

This is a supplication for guidance, forgiveness, knowledge, provision, patience in their trial, steadfastness, strength, security, and eventual deliverance. They prayed that the end of their affair would be sound and rightly guided. In times of difficulty and ambiguity, two of the most important things to ask for are mercy and guidance. Through Allah's infinite mercy the

46 There are several opinions regarding the exact meaning of "raqīm." For example, some mention that it is the name of a book that contains laws and teachings related to Christianity. Others suggest that it's the name of the valley, mountain, or region in which the cave is located. Some others say that it's the name of a monument or building that was constructed to commemorate their story, the name of their leader, the name of their dog, or the name of the town that they fled from. I have chosen the meaning that most of the commentators have adopted, which is that it refers to an inscription made on a tablet placed at the entrance of the cave that details their story.

difficulty will be made easy and through His guidance things will become clear.

Allah ﷻ responded to their supplication by causing them to sleep for a long period of time. “So We drew a veil over their ears in the cave, for a number of years...” This is an Arabic expression that means He put them into a very deep sleep. “And then We awakened them so that We could make clear which of the two parties was better able to calculate how long they had remained in that state.” In this verse “the two parties” is referring to two groups that differed over the length of time the youth had remained asleep in the cave[47]. The two groups could be referring to two groups among the sleepers themselves, the sleepers and the people of the city, or anyone who differed regarding their matter. Here, Allah ﷻ is mentioning one of the reasons why He miraculously awakened the sleeping youth after such a long period of time; in order to show which of the two groups was closer to the truth.

After this brief summary that captures our interest, the Sūrah begins a more detailed narrative by stating that what is about to be mentioned is the truth regarding their affair.

نَّحْنُ نَقُصُّ عَلَيْكَ نَبَأَهُم بِالْحَقِّ ۚ إِنَّهُمْ فِتْيَةٌ آمَنُوا بِرَبِّهِمْ
وَزِدْنَاهُمْ هُدًى ﴿١٣﴾

13 We relate to you their story in truth. They were young men who believed in their Lord, so We increased them in guidance.

47 See verse 22

Allah ﷻ is telling us that He will relate the real and true story to us; not the exaggerated or false version that was preserved by the people of that time. This event took place between the time of Īsā ﷺ and Muḥammad ﷺ. The People of the Cave were from a city known as Ephesus (Ufsūs in Arabic), which was a major city in the Roman Empire. It is located on the west coast of Asia Minor.[48] The people and government of the Roman Empire at that time were idol worshippers. Their society had reached the heights of moral decay and immorality. It was a society built on vice, materialism, immorality, ignorance, and disbelief. The Emperor's name during that time is mentioned as Daqyānūs (Decius). He was an oppressive tyrant forcing his people to worship idols. This was a time when Christians were being persecuted for their religious beliefs.

Every year the people would take part in a religious festival where they would meet to worship and sacrifice on behalf of their idols. One year, the seven young men, identified as the people of the cave[49], came to the festival. They were shocked by what they saw; people taking rocks that they carved with their own hands as gods, worshipping them, and sacrificing for them. Allah ﷻ blessed them to dislike and turn away from this absurd behavior. They used their reason and intellect to arrive at the logical conclusion that worship belongs to the Supreme Being Who has created the heavens and the earth and everything in them.

"They were young men who believed in their Lord, so We increased them in guidance." Allah ﷻ highlights the fact that they were youth. That's because being young is a virtue; there are certain advantages to it. Generally speaking, when a person is young they are more inquisitive, open-minded, impressionable, courageous, brave, and strong. They are still shaping who they are as a person and formulating their thoughts, ideas, beliefs, personality, and identity. Even historically it was the youth of a community who

---

48 This is the most likely geographical information regarding the People of the Cave according to several Tafsīr authorities. There are other opinions mentioned and it is difficult to determine the definitive location of the cave; it could be in Andalus, Jordan, or Turkey. The speculative nature of the geographical information does not affect the Quranic narrative because understanding the verses and their lessons is not dependent upon this information. Ibn Kathīr ﷺ says, "And He did not tell us about the location of this cave in a particular city because there is no benefit or religious objective in knowing so."

49 There are narrations that mention their names; however, Imām al-Qurṭubī mentions that all of these narrations are extremely weak and unreliable.

responded to the message of the Prophets, while the elders were more entrenched and set in their ways. It was the younger members of Quraysh that were more open and willing to listen to and follow the Prophet ﷺ. The individuals in this story were youth who believed in the existence, oneness, might, and power of their Lord. As a result of this firm belief and conviction, Allah ﷻ guided them towards what was best for them in terms of this life and the next. He increased them in guidance by strengthening their faith, facilitating righteous deeds for them, enabling them to dedicate themselves to worship, and detach themselves from the material.

This thought, the absurdity of their people's beliefs, crossed their minds at the same time and they all started moving away from the festival. The first young man went far away from the crowd and sat down under a tree. Then the second and the third also did the same until all seven of them gathered at that tree. None of them were familiar with each other, nor did they know why they had all gathered at the same spot. After sitting there silently, one of them finally spoke up and explained why he had come to sit under the tree. They all started talking and discussing and came to the same conclusion. So they broke away from the way of their people, rejecting their way of life and system of belief. They set up their own place of worship where they would get together to worship Allah ﷻ. However, they soon became the talk of the town. Their news spread throughout the city. The Emperor learned about them and had them arrested and brought before him. He asked them about their beliefs.[50] Allah ﷻ gave them the strength and courage to state their belief in the Oneness of God. They even called the Emperor towards the message of tawḥīd.

50 ibn Kathīr, *Tafsīr al-Quran al-ʿAẓīm*, 9:110-111

VERSE 14

وَرَبَطْنَا عَلَىٰ قُلُوبِهِمْ إِذْ قَامُوا فَقَالُوا رَبُّنَا رَبُّ السَّمَاوَاتِ وَالْأَرْضِ
لَن نَّدْعُوَ مِن دُونِهِ إِلَٰهًا ۖ لَّقَدْ قُلْنَا إِذًا شَطَطًا ﴿١٤﴾

14 And We fortified their hearts when they stood up and said, "Our Lord is the Lord of the heavens and the earth. We will never call upon any god besides Him, for then we would have certainly uttered an outrage.

"And We fortified their hearts" means that Allah ﷻ gave them the courage, confidence, patience, and strength to speak the truth in front of the Emperor. This verse highlights their open defiance to the tyrant Emperor. They stood up and courageously spoke the truth despite the fear of persecution. They knew that if they spoke the truth in front of the Emperor they would be in trouble, but that didn't stop them. Their faith was strong and as a result, Allah ﷻ strengthened their hearts and resolve giving them courage to speak truth to power. Courage is related to faith; the stronger a person's īmān is, the more courageous they will be. Speaking truth to power is a very important concept in Islam. The Prophet ﷺ told us, "The best form of jihad is to speak the truth in front of a tyrant ruler."[51]

They told him, "Our Lord is the Lord of the heavens and the earth. We will never call upon any god besides Him, for then we would have certainly uttered an outrage." They declared their belief in very clear and straightforward words. They professed their belief in the existence and oneness of Allah ﷻ, Who created the heavens and the earth and everything they contain.

51 Abū Dāwūd, *k. al-malāḥim*, *b. al-amr wa al-nahy*, 4344

They also declared that they would devote their worship and servitude to Him alone. They recognized that calling upon anyone other than God and worshipping someone or something other than Him is an "outrage." This angered the Emperor even more. He gave them a few days to reconsider their beliefs and to return to the way of the people. If they did, they would be allowed to live. If not, then he would kill them. These few days were a blessing from Allah ﷻ that provided them the opportunity to further strengthen their faith and to escape from the city and find safety and refuge in a cave.

VERSE 15

هَٰٓؤُلَآءِ قَوْمُنَا ٱتَّخَذُوا۟ مِن دُونِهِۦٓ ءَالِهَةً ۖ لَّوْلَا يَأْتُونَ عَلَيْهِم بِسُلْطَٰنٍۭ
بَيِّنٍ ۖ فَمَنْ أَظْلَمُ مِمَّنِ ٱفْتَرَىٰ عَلَى ٱللَّهِ كَذِبًا ﴿١٥﴾

15 These, our people, have taken gods other than Him. Why do they not bring a clear proof concerning them? For who does greater wrong than the one who fabricates a lie against Allah?

The people of the cave are highlighting the main issue they had with the religion and way of life of their people, which is taking others as deities besides the One and True Creator. They recognized the absurdity of associating partners with Allah ﷻ. If these idols are truly worthy of worship, then why don't they provide some sort of proof or evidence? Why don't they produce some sort of rational or observational proof to support their claims and beliefs? They recognized that what their nation was involved in is one of the greatest wrongs that can be done against Allah ﷻ. That's why they ask, "Who does greater wrong than the one who fabricates a lie against Allah?" This is a rhetorical question that means there is no one who does a greater wrong than fabricating a lie against Allah ﷻ.

Syed Quṭb ﷺ comments, "Up to this point the attitude of the youths appears to be clear, open, and straightforward. They are resolute in their adoption of the faith, betraying no hesitation whatsoever. Indeed they are shown to be very strong physically and mentally, and strong in their faith and in their rejection of the way followed by their community. Here they are talking about two vastly different ways of life. There can be no meeting point between the two, and there can be no participation by these young believers in the life of their community. They had no choice but to flee in order to protect their faith."[52]

They escaped from their town and sought refuge in a cave in order to protect their faith and religion. They left the comfort of their homes, the only way of life they knew, their families, belongings, and their friends, just for the sake of their religion. They gave up all pleasures of this life for the sake of Allah ﷻ. Sometimes our faith will require us to make sacrifices; emotional, physical, and financial. Allah ﷻ then tells us what they said to each other once they decided to flee.

وَإِذِ اعْتَزَلْتُمُوهُمْ وَمَا يَعْبُدُونَ إِلَّا اللَّهَ فَأْوُوا إِلَى الْكَهْفِ يَنشُرْ لَكُمْ رَبُّكُم مِّن رَّحْمَتِهِ وَيُهَيِّئْ لَكُم مِّنْ أَمْرِكُم مِّرْفَقًا ﴿١٦﴾

[16] When you have turned away from them, and those whom

52 Quṭb, *fī Ẓilāl al-Quran*, 4:2262

they worship, except Allah, then seek refuge in the cave, and your Lord will extend His mercy for you, and provide you ease in your matters.

Some of the commentators mention that these are the words of the leader of the youths, which he said when they decided to flee for the sake of their religion. He told them that once they totally abandon the beliefs of their people and devote themselves in worship, servitude, and submission to Allah ﷻ alone, He will take care of them. That once they seek refuge in the cave in order to protect their beliefs, Allah ﷻ would shower His mercy upon them and make their affairs easy for them.

In this statement he's reminding them to rely upon Allah ﷻ and to place their trust fully in Him. If you place your trust in Allah ﷻ and rely solely upon Him, He will take care of you. He will shower His infinite mercy upon you, protect you, and make your affairs easy. Īmān is extremely powerful. It is something real, observable, and alive. It is something that can be felt and experienced. Īmān exhibits itself through a person's speech, behavior, conduct, the way they carry themselves, their morals, values, ethics, and principles. It is meant to change our perspective of the world. When a human heart is full of faith, it sees a totally different world, where Allah's infinite mercy creates reassurance and genuine happiness. It makes every difficulty and challenge seem easy. It provides us with the tools and attitude to navigate through whatever challenges life sends our way and this is exactly what we see here in the story of these young men.

They were truly people of tawakkul. Tawakkul is perhaps one of the most powerful characteristics that we can have; it's the key to true happiness. It is the foundation of a worry-free, stress-free, anxiety-free life. It leads to a life of peace and contentment. Linguistically the word التَّوَكُّل is a verbal noun from the verb تَوَكَّل/يَتَوَكَّل, which means to rely, depend on, to place one's confidence in or to trust. It's derived from the root letters و ك ل that convey the meaning of relying upon someone else for something. One who relies on Allah ﷻ, who has التوكل on Allah ﷻ, is the one who knows that Allah ﷻ takes care of his sustenance and affairs, so he trusts Allah ﷻ alone and doesn't rely on anyone else. It's having absolute, firm, one hundred percent conviction that no one gives, prevents, harms or benefits except for Allah ﷻ. The reality of tawakkul is that we place our trust and reliance on Allah ﷻ in terms of both our worldly affairs, as well as our dīn, as well as utilising our visceral, or tangible means of attaining that which we want.

Once they reached the cave, Allah ﷻ put them to sleep, "So We placed [a veil] over their ears in the cave for a number of years." Allah ﷻ, as a sign of His great power and majesty, kept them asleep for 309 years. They literally disappeared from the face of the earth; they were nowhere to be found. The king wrote down their names on a tablet so that they wouldn't be forgotten and had it saved for future reference. The next few verses inform us of what happened to them in the cave as a sign and proof of the infinite might and power of Allah ﷻ. Allah ﷻ provides details regarding their long sleep, of how He protected their bodies and kept them alive without any food and drink, and protected them from being found.

VERSES 17-18

وَتَرَى الشَّمْسَ إِذَا طَلَعَت تَّزَاوَرُ عَن كَهْفِهِمْ ذَاتَ الْيَمِينِ وَإِذَا
غَرَبَت تَّقْرِضُهُمْ ذَاتَ الشِّمَالِ وَهُمْ فِي فَجْوَةٍ مِّنْهُ ۚ ذَٰلِكَ مِنْ
آيَاتِ اللَّهِ ۗ مَن يَهْدِ اللَّهُ فَهُوَ الْمُهْتَدِ ۖ وَمَن يُضْلِلْ فَلَن تَجِدَ
لَهُ وَلِيًّا مُّرْشِدًا ﴿١٧﴾ وَتَحْسَبُهُمْ أَيْقَاظًا وَهُمْ رُقُودٌ ۚ وَنُقَلِّبُهُمْ ذَاتَ
الْيَمِينِ وَذَاتَ الشِّمَالِ ۖ وَكَلْبُهُم بَاسِطٌ ذِرَاعَيْهِ بِالْوَصِيدِ ۚ لَوِ
اطَّلَعْتَ عَلَيْهِمْ لَوَلَّيْتَ مِنْهُمْ فِرَارًا وَلَمُلِئْتَ مِنْهُمْ رُعْبًا ﴿١٨﴾

17 You would see the sun, when it rose, turning away from their cave towards the right; and when it set, it bypassed them towards the left, while they were in an open space

within it. That is one of the signs of Allah. Whomsoever Allah guides, he is rightly guided; and whomsoever He lets go astray, for him you will find no one to help, no one to lead. [18] And you would think they were awake while they were asleep. We turned them on their sides, right and left. And their dog had its forelegs stretched out to the doorstep. If you had a look at them, you would have fled away from them and would have been filled with awe of them.

According to most commentators, these verses are being addressed to the Prophet ﷺ providing him with unique details of their condition within the cave that could only be known through revelation. This is actually an amazing scene being described to us by Allah ﷻ.

"You would see the sun, when it rose, turning away from their cave towards the right; and when it set, it bypassed them towards the left." The sun would pass by them in the morning and evening, but would not shine directly on their bodies as a favor from Allah ﷻ. This kept the environment, temperature, and moisture of the cave ideal. This is perhaps one of the apparent ways in which their bodies and clothes were preserved.

"While they were in an open space within it." They were in "an open space within it," meaning that the cave was spacious, allowing for fresh air and cool breeze to reach them as they slept. "That is one of the signs of Allah." Allah ﷻ tells us that the sun passing by them in the morning and evening, while not shining directly on their bodies is one the many signs of His infinite might, power, wisdom, magnificence, and glory. It shows that Allah ﷻ protects those who turn to Him with sincerity.

Allah ﷻ concludes the verse saying, "Whomsoever Allah guides, he is rightly guided; and whomsoever He lets go astray, for him you will find no one to help, no one to lead." Here Allah ﷻ is highlighting the concepts of hidāyah and ḍalālah, guidance and misguidance. If a person is sincerely searching for the truth, Allah ﷻ will open up the path for their guidance. Allah ﷻ will open their hearts and minds and guide them towards the truth. When He allows a person to go astray, it is a consequence of their own poor choices, decisions, and actions. "There is a certain divine law that determines which people may receive God's guidance and which are left in error. When a person looks at God's signs and accepts what they indicate, that person finds God's guidance in accordance with His law. Hence, he is 'indeed rightly guided.' (Verse 17) But whoever turns his back on these signs and refuses to understand the message they impart is bound, according to God's law, to go astray. Hence he is left in error and will have none to guide him."[53] This is also a source of consolation and comfort for the Prophet ﷺ reminding him that his responsibility is to simply convey the message while guidance is the realm of Allah ﷻ.

Allah ﷻ then continues describing their condition and state in the cave saying, "And you would think they were awake while they were asleep." They didn't look like they were asleep. Anyone who looked at them would think that they were awake. Some commentators mention that perhaps they were made to sleep with their eyes open so if anyone were to come across them it would look like they were awake.

"We turned them on their sides, right and left." This is another expression of Allah's infinite grace and mercy upon them. As they slept for hundreds of years, Allah ﷻ caused them to change sides and positions. This was done to avoid harm being done to their bodies in the appearance of sores.

"And their dog had its forelegs stretched out to the doorstep." This dog belonged to one of the young men and he had brought it along with them to the cave. The dog was also put to sleep for this long period of time and because of the way it was positioned it seemed like it was guarding them. It was sleeping at the entrance of the cave in the position of a guard dog. Dogs are very unique animals and are considered to be extremely loyal. This particular dog was so special and loyal that Allah ﷻ mentions it in His last and final revelation.

Some of the scholars of the Quran mention that one of the lessons we can learn from this is how people can benefit from the company of the righteous. Ibn Aṭiyah said, "Truly those who love the righteous will receive some of their blessings. A dog that loved the people of virtue and accompanied them, Allah ﷻ mentions it in His revelation."[54] Imām al-Qurṭubī remarks that if a dog was able to earn such an honor by being in the company of the righteous, then what do you think about believers who love and interact with the pious and righteous. Anas ؓ narrates that a person came to Allah's Messenger ﷺ

53 Quṭb, *fī Ẓilāl al-Quran*, 4:2263

54 Qurṭubī, *al-Jāmiʿ li Aḥkām al-Quran*, 13:231

and asked, "When is the Hour? The Prophet ﷺ responded, "What have you prepared for it?" He said, "Love for Allah and of His Messenger." The Prophet ﷺ said, "Truly you are with the one you love." Anas رضي الله عنه then said, "Nothing pleased us more after accepting Islam than the words of Allah's Apostle "you are with the one you love." He also said, "I love Allah and His Messenger and Abū Bakr and Umar, and I hope that I would be with them although I have not acted like them."[55]

Allah ﷻ continues describing how they were sleeping in the cave, "If you had a look at them, you would have fled away from them and would have been filled with awe of them." If someone were to come across them and look at them they would become scared and run away. All of this was done by Allah ﷻ, according to His divine wisdom, to protect them until a time He chose for them to wake up.

وَكَذَٰلِكَ بَعَثْنَاهُمْ لِيَتَسَاءَلُوا بَيْنَهُمْ ۚ قَالَ قَائِلٌ مِّنْهُمْ كَمْ لَبِثْتُمْ ۖ
قَالُوا لَبِثْنَا يَوْمًا أَوْ بَعْضَ يَوْمٍ ۚ قَالُوا رَبُّكُمْ أَعْلَمُ بِمَا لَبِثْتُمْ
فَابْعَثُوا أَحَدَكُم بِوَرِقِكُمْ هَٰذِهِ إِلَى الْمَدِينَةِ فَلْيَنظُرْ أَيُّهَا أَزْكَىٰ
طَعَامًا فَلْيَأْتِكُم بِرِزْقٍ مِّنْهُ وَلْيَتَلَطَّفْ وَلَا يُشْعِرَنَّ بِكُمْ
أَحَدًا ﴿١٩﴾ إِنَّهُمْ إِن يَظْهَرُوا عَلَيْكُمْ يَرْجُمُوكُمْ أَوْ يُعِيدُوكُمْ فِي
مِلَّتِهِمْ وَلَن تُفْلِحُوا إِذًا أَبَدًا ﴿٢٠﴾

[19] And in this way We raised them up until they asked each

55 Muslim, *k. al-birr wa al-ṣilah wa al-ādāb, b. al-mar' maʿā man aḥabb*, 2639

other. One of them said, "How long have you been here?" They said, "A day, or part of a day." They said, "Your Lord knows best how long you have remained. So, send one of you with this silver (coin) of yours to the city and let him observe which of them has the purest food and bring you some provision therefrom. Let him be discreet and make no one aware of you. [20] Verily, if they come to know about you, they will stone you, or make you revert to their faith, and in that case, you will never find success."

"And in this way We raised them up." Just as Allah ﷻ had miraculously caused them to go to sleep for hundreds of years in such a unique, strange, and miraculous way, Allah ﷻ also woke them up miraculously from their slumber. Allah ﷻ woke them up after 309 years, healthy and fit without having eaten or drunken anything. Once they woke up, they started asking each other how long they had been sleeping for. One of them asked, "How long have you remained [asleep]?" Since they were completely unaware of how long they had been sleeping for, some of them said perhaps a day or even just part of a day. Some versions of the story mention that they thought they had only been asleep for a day or part of a day because when they went to sleep it was the morning and when they woke up it was the evening. But after looking at their appearance they figured that something strange had happened; their hair and nails were extremely long. They concluded that Allah ﷻ knows best how long they had been asleep for. "Your Lord knows best how long you have remained."

"So, send one of you with this silver (coin) of yours to the city and let him observe which of them has the purest food and bring you some provision therefrom." After having slept for such a long period of time they were extremely hungry, so they chose one person to send to the city to get food. They sent him with some silver coins to go buy food from the city that was pure, wholesome, and lawful according to them. The silver coins that they had were from the era of the oppressive king and still had his imprint. They also told him to be extremely careful, to be discreet, so that no one finds out who he is. "Let him be discreet and make no one aware of you." They thought that they were still living in the same time period of religious persecution and if the people of the city found out about them they would either kill them or force them to worship idols. They feared that if the people found out about them they would be persecuted. "Verily, if they come to know about you, they will stone you, or make you revert to their faith, and in that case, you will never find success." They were unaware that things had changed drastically since they had fallen asleep.

The Sūrah now skips a few scenes from the story and tells us what happened when the people came to find out about them.

وَكَذَٰلِكَ أَعْثَرْنَا عَلَيْهِمْ لِيَعْلَمُوا أَنَّ وَعْدَ اللَّهِ حَقٌّ وَأَنَّ السَّاعَةَ لَا
رَيْبَ فِيهَا إِذْ يَتَنَازَعُونَ بَيْنَهُمْ أَمْرَهُمْ ۖ فَقَالُوا ابْنُوا عَلَيْهِم بُنْيَانًا ۖ
رَّبُّهُمْ أَعْلَمُ بِهِمْ ۚ قَالَ الَّذِينَ غَلَبُوا عَلَىٰ أَمْرِهِمْ لَنَتَّخِذَنَّ عَلَيْهِم
مَّسْجِدًا ﴿٢١﴾

[21] And in this way, We made them known to the people (of the city), so that they realize that Allah's promise is true, and that there is no doubt about the Hour (the Day of Resurrection). When they were disputing among themselves in their matter, they said, "Erect a building over them. Their Lord knows them best." Said those who prevailed in their matter, "We will certainly make a mosque over them."

During the 309 years that Allah ﷻ miraculously kept them asleep, the city they were from changed completely. It was no longer a city of idol worshippers; the majority of people had become Christian. The Emperor was also a righteous man. Their story also became somewhat of folklore and was passed on from generation to generation.

Unaware of how drastically things had changed this person went to the city with his ancient clothes and his ancient money. He was unknowingly attracting attention towards himself because of his strange appearance. Then when he tried to purchase some food he took out these ancient silver coins and attracted even more attention. The people of the town recognized that something was wrong; there was something unique about this person, so they detained him and took him to the Emperor.

It just so happened that during this time there was a huge theological debate regarding the concept of resurrection; will both body and soul be resurrected or just the soul? There were a group of people who believed that resurrection was purely spiritual, while another group along with the emperor believed that it was both physical and spiritual. When they brought the young man before him he began to question him and figured out that he was one of the people of the cave that they had heard about from their parents and grandparents. This made him extremely happy as it was the definitive proof needed to settle their theological debate regarding resurrection.

The king then took a delegation back to the cave. Some versions of the story mention that the king and his delegation spoke briefly with the people of the cave after which they went back to sleep and finally passed away. In this way, Allah ﷻ caused "them to be known to the people (of the city), so that they realize that Allah's promise is true, and that there is no doubt about the Hour (the Day of Resurrection)." Allah ﷻ Himself mentions two specific reasons or wisdoms behind allowing the people of the cave to sleep for so long and then waking them from their slumber. One is so that the people of that time specifically, and those after them generally, will know with absolute certainty that Allah's promise is true. Allah's promise to bring the dead back to life and help, aid, assist, and support the believers is the absolute truth. The second reason or wisdom is so "that there is no doubt about the Hour." One who has the ability to cause people to sleep for centuries and then wake them up unaltered can certainly raise the dead. "The end these young people met shows a real, tangible example of how resurrection takes place.

The people in the city felt the full impact of resurrection and realized, as they could never have done otherwise, that God's promise in respect of resurrection after death will come true and that the Last Hour is certain to come."[56]

Afterwards, the people of the town started disputing amongst themselves on how to commemorate these youth; what's the proper way of celebrating and preserving their legacy? They split into two groups. One group suggested "erect a building over them" and the other decided that it was better to erect a place of worship. "Those who prevailed over their affair," meaning those who were either more in number or whose opinion carried more weight, said, "We shall build a place of worship over them.'" So a place of worship was built next to their cave in order to commemorate them as was the practice of Jews and Christians of that time.

This was an amazing incident that took place in history. As time went on and the story was passed on from generation to generation the story started to change; sometimes people added certain details and others omitted some. As time went on people started arguing and debating over the exact details of the story; specifically how many youth there were in the cave. Allah ﷻ tells us,

سَيَقُولُونَ ثَلَاثَةٌ رَّابِعُهُمْ كَلْبُهُمْ وَيَقُولُونَ خَمْسَةٌ سَادِسُهُمْ كَلْبُهُمْ
رَجْمًا بِالْغَيْبِ ۖ وَيَقُولُونَ سَبْعَةٌ وَثَامِنُهُمْ كَلْبُهُمْ ۚ قُل رَّبِّي أَعْلَمُ
بِعِدَّتِهِم مَّا يَعْلَمُهُمْ إِلَّا قَلِيلٌ ۗ فَلَا تُمَارِ فِيهِمْ إِلَّا مِرَاءً ظَاهِرًا
وَلَا تَسْتَفْتِ فِيهِم مِّنْهُمْ أَحَدًا ﴿٢٢﴾

56 Quṭb, *fī Ẓilāl al-Quran*, 4:2264

[22] They will say, "(They were) three, and the fourth was their dog." And they will say, "Five, and the sixth was their dog," guessing at the unseen. And they will say, "Seven, and the eight was their dog." Say, "My Lord knows best about their number." No one knows them except a few, so do not argue about them except an apparent argumentation, nor consult any of them about them.

What we learn from this verse is that with the passage of time there was a debate and discussion regarding the exact number of people inside of the cave. Allah ﷻ is telling us that people disputed over the number of the people in the cave. The verse mentions three opinions:

1. Three people along with their dog
2. Five people along with their dog
3. Seven people along with their dog

Allah ﷻ uses language that indicates that the first two opinions were incorrect because He ﷻ says, "Guessing at the unseen." Meaning, they were simply guessing and speaking without knowledge. After mentioning the last opinion, the verse neither confirms it nor rejects it. That is why most commentators interpret that to mean that this last opinion is correct. This is also the opinion of ibn Abbās ؓ, who is considered to be the most knowledgeable companion of the Prophet ﷺ in terms of understanding the Quran.

Allah ﷻ then tells the Prophet ﷺ to say, "My Lord knows best about their number." Meaning, the best thing to do in matters like this - matters in which there is no definitive knowledge - is to refer their knowledge to Allah ﷻ. Simply say, "Allah ﷻ knows best." There's no need to discuss issues without having any knowledge and speak based on pure conjecture. Speaking about Allah ﷻ, His Messenger ﷺ, and His religion without sound knowledge is extremely dangerous. As a matter of fact, there are several warnings from the Prophet ﷺ against doing so. There is absolutely no shame or embarrassment whatsoever in saying, "I don't know" or "Allah knows best." Ibn Umar ؓ said, "Knowledge is of three types: a speaking book (the Quran), an established Sunnah, and I don't know."[57] This is especially true for scholars and people of knowledge. If they are asked regarding something which they don't know or are unsure they should say, "I don't know," "I haven't researched it," or "Allah knows best." This is a sign of true knowledge, understanding, sincerity, and God-consciousness.

Allah then tells us, "No one knows them except a few." Meaning, that there were a few people who knew their number and other details of the story based on sound knowledge. Ibn 'Abbās used to say, "I am one of the few mentioned in this verse; they were seven."[58]

The verse ends by addressing the Prophet, "So do not argue about them except an apparent argumentation. And do not ask anyone of these about them." Allah is instructing him not to debate with people regarding this matter but to rather let the parts of the story that have been revealed to him suffice. The "apparent argument" is referring to the details of their narrative that have been revealed to the Prophet. One of the most important lessons and morals from this verse is not to get into discussions that are neither important nor necessary. What's important here isn't their specific number; rather, what is important are the lessons and morals that can be derived from their story.

Allah now reminds the Prophet that he shouldn't say he will do or say something in the future without acknowledging that its fulfillment depends upon the will of Allah.

وَلَا تَقُولَنَّ لِشَيْءٍ إِنِّي فَاعِلٌ ذَٰلِكَ غَدًا ﴿٢٣﴾ إِلَّا أَن يَشَاءَ اللَّهُ ۚ وَاذْكُر

57 Haythamī, *Majmaʿ al-Zawāʾid*, 1:177

58 Qurṭubī, *al-Jāmiʿ li Aḥkām al-Quran*, 13:248

رَّبَّكَ إِذَا نَسِيتَ وَقُلْ عَسَىٰٓ أَن يَهْدِيَنِ رَبِّى لِأَقْرَبَ مِنْ هَٰذَا رَشَدًا ﴿٢٤﴾

[23] And don't say about anything, "I will surely do it tomorrow," [24] without saying, "If Allah wills." And remember your Lord if you forget and say, "It may be that my Lord will guide me to what is more right than this."

In order to understand these verses properly, it is important to keep the cause of revelation of this Sūrah in mind. It was mentioned earlier that the Prophet ﷺ was asked three questions - the story of the youth, the soul, and Dhū al-Qarnayn - by the leadership of Quraysh and he said he will inform them about what they're asking tomorrow, but he forgot to say, "in shā'a Allah," meaning, "If Allah wills." As a gentle reminder for the Prophet ﷺ and as a lesson for his Companions ﷺ and those that come after, revelation was delayed for several days. These verses are addressed directly to the Prophet ﷺ, and through them Allah ﷻ is reminding him, and by extension all believers, that they shouldn't intend to do something in the near or distant future without acknowledging that its fulfillment depends upon the will of Allah ﷻ. Meaning, whenever we intend to do something we should say, "If Allah wills." That's why it's a regular practice in Muslim societies throughout the world to use this phrase very often. This verse serves as a constant reminder that nothing in this universe happens without the will, command, and decree of Allah ﷻ.

Syed Quṭb beautifully writes, "Every action a human being does or omits to do, indeed every breath a human being takes, is subject to God's will. The curtains hiding the future are stretched in full so as to hide everything beyond the present moment. Our eyes cannot discern what is behind that curtain, and our minds are finite, no matter how advanced our knowledge may be. Hence, a human being must never say that he is definitely doing something tomorrow, unless he attaches his intention to God's will. This is because tomorrow belongs to the realm that lies beyond the reach of human perception. As such, it is known only to God. Hence, we do not make any assertion about it.

This does not mean that man should be fatalistic, giving no thought to the future and making no plans for it. He should not live for the present moment, cutting himself off from his past and future. No, this is not what the directive implies. Rather, what is implied is that every human being must make an allowance for what God may will in his case. He may intend to do whatever he wants, always seeking God's help, feeling that His will is in full control of everything. It may well be however that God may decide something different to what he intends. Should God help him to put into effect what he intends, then all well and good. But if God's will moves in a different direction, he should not despair or be sad. All matters belong to God at the beginning and at the end.

What this means in practice is that every person should think and plan as they wish, but they must always remember to rely on God's help and guidance. They should realize that they only have the faculties of thinking and deliberation God has given them. This should not lead to laziness or disinterestedness. On the contrary, it should give us more strength, confidence, reassurance and resolve. Should events reveal that God's will has moved in a direction different to what we planned, we should accept this with contentment and reassurance. We submit to God's will, because it is beyond our knowledge until God makes it known."[59]

Allah ﷻ then tells us what to do if we forget to say "if Allah wills." "And remember your Lord if you forget and say, 'It may be that my Lord will guide me to what is more right than this'." If a person forgets to say in shā'a Allah, they should remember Allah ﷻ and renew their reliance upon Him. They should supplicate to Allah ﷻ asking Him to guide them towards rushd - understanding, perception, insight, and the ability to see and recognize the truth. The guidance being provided here by Allah ﷻ is that if we forget to mention His name, we shouldn't feel sorrow and regret. We should simply renew our connection with Him ﷻ by mentioning His name and supplicating to Him saying, "It may be that my Lord will guide me to what is more right than this."

---

59 Quṭb, *fī Ẓilāl al-Quran*, 4:2265

VERSES 25-26

وَلَبِثُوا فِي كَهْفِهِمْ ثَلَاثَ مِائَةٍ سِنِينَ وَازْدَادُوا تِسْعًا ﴿٢٥﴾ قُلِ اللَّهُ
أَعْلَمُ بِمَا لَبِثُوا ۖ لَهُ غَيْبُ السَّمَاوَاتِ وَالْأَرْضِ ۖ أَبْصِرْ بِهِ وَأَسْمِعْ ۚ
مَا لَهُم مِّن دُونِهِ مِن وَلِيٍّ وَلَا يُشْرِكُ فِي حُكْمِهِ أَحَدًا ﴿٢٦﴾

[25] And they remained in their cave for three hundred years, plus nine more. [26] Say, "Allah knows best how long they stayed. To Him belongs the unseen of the heavens and the earth. How well He sees, how well He hears! They have no guardian besides Him, and He makes no one a partner with Him in His judgment."

Allah ﷻ informs us how long they remained sleeping in the cave. He ﷻ tells us that they remained sleeping for 309 years.[60] "And they remained in their cave for three hundred years, plus nine more." This definitive knowledge settled any disputes that may have existed regarding this particular detail of their story. That is one of the reasons why Allah ﷻ then tells the Prophet ﷺ to relegate the knowledge of the exact details to Allah ﷻ. "Say, 'Allah knows best how long they stayed. To Him belongs the unseen of the heavens and the earth." This is a reminder of Allah's infinite and limitless knowledge. Allah ﷻ is al-Alīm, the All-Knowing, whose knowledge encompasses every single thing big or small, unseen and seen, private and public, internal and external. He ﷻ alone knows the unseen of

60 According to ibn Kathīr ﷺ this is referring to lunar years. In solar years it was 300 years.

the heavens and the earth.

Not only is Allah ﷻ the All-Knowing, but He is also the All-Seeing, al-Baṣīr, and the All-Hearing, al-Samī. "How well He sees, how well He hears!" is a particular construction that conveys the meaning of amazement and exaggeration. Allah ﷻ sees every single thing that happens in this universe and hears every single sound; absolutely nothing is hidden from Him.

Allah ﷻ concludes the passage with two remarks regarding His oneness. "They have no guardian besides Him, and He makes no one a partner with Him in His judgment." Allah ﷻ alone is the guardian and protector of all of mankind taking care of all of their affairs. There is no other deity, being, or object that can provide protection by bringing benefit and preventing harm. He ﷻ alone is the One who decrees every single thing that happens in this universe. Every single detail in this universe is under the command, control, will, and decree of Allah ﷻ.

LESSONS FROM THE STORY OF THE PEOPLE OF THE CAVE

There are several lessons, morals, reminders, and guidance that can be derived from the story of the people of the cave.

1.

This story serves as consolation, comfort, and support for the Prophet ﷺ, his companions, and us as believers. Trials, tests, challenges, and difficulties, particularly those related to belief and practice, are part of the human experience. This story provides us with insight on how to navigate through these challenges and overcome them with courage, patience, and reliance upon Allah ﷻ.

2.

The story serves as a proof of prophethood and the miraculous nature of the Quran – the only way possible for the Prophet ﷺ to know these details regarding their story was through revelation. This is part of the miraculous nature of the Quran.

3.

It serves as proof of the infinite might, power, glory, and magnificence of Allah ﷻ, as well as proof of resurrection. It is among the "signs" of Allah ﷻ that indicate towards His existence, oneness, and power that serve as a means to strengthen our faith and relationship with Allah ﷻ. There are also symbolic parallels between their story, death, and resurrection.

4.

It highlights the importance of having genuine care and concern for the protection of one's faith and religion.

5.

It is an excellent example of being dedicated to faith and religion in one's youth. There is a well-known ḥadīth of the Prophet ﷺ in which he mentions seven groups of people who will be shaded on the Day of Judgment. One of them is a youth who was brought up and nurtured in the worship of Allah.[61]

6.

There's a unique relationship between youth, faith, and bringing about change in society.

7.

It highlights the importance of righteous companionship.

8.

Faith (īmān), reliance upon Allah ﷻ (tawakkul), and patience (ṣabr) have a direct relationship with Allah's mercy, care, and protection.

9.

The story highlights the concepts of guidance (hidāyah) and misguidance (ḍalālah).

---

61 Muslim, *k. al-zakāh, b. faḍl ikhfā'a al-ṣadaqah*, 1031

10.

We can draw several parallels between their seeking refuge in the cave and the Prophet ﷺ and Abū Bakr ؓ seeking refuge in the cave during migration.

11.

It is a practical example of speaking truth to power.

12.

The importance of avoiding useless discussions that have no relevance or importance to one's life, salvation, faith or relationship with Allah ﷻ.

13.

Don't discuss topics without knowledge!

14.

The importance of saying, "in shā'a Allah" and recognizing that everything happens according to the will, decree, judgment, and wisdom of Allah ﷻ.

The next set of verses deal with issues of general guidance in a very beautiful way. Allah ﷻ says,

وَاتْلُ مَا أُوحِيَ إِلَيْكَ مِن كِتَابِ رَبِّكَ ۖ لَا مُبَدِّلَ لِكَلِمَاتِهِ وَلَن
تَجِدَ مِن دُونِهِ مُلْتَحَدًا ﴿٢٧﴾

27 Recite what has been revealed to you from the book of your Lord. There is nothing that can alter His words. And you will never find refuge other than with Him.

In this verse, Allah ﷻ is speaking directly to the Prophet ﷺ. He's instructing His Messenger to continue to recite the noble Quran and remain steadfast in conveying its message to his community. He ﷻ commands him to recite what has been revealed to him and follow what is in it in terms of its commands, prohibitions, recommendations, and guidance. This was one of the responsibilities of the Prophet ﷺ as a Prophet and Messenger; to recite the actual words of revelation to his community. To convey the word of God to his family, friends, neighbors, and all of society. And when the Prophet ﷺ would do so, he would face all sorts of challenges. Some people would turn away and others would mock and ridicule him. They would even ask him to bring a different Quran or to alter it according to their wishes.

As a response Allah ﷻ reminds them, "There is nothing that can alter His words." The Quran is divinely protected as Allah ﷻ says in Sūrah al-Ḥijr, "It is certainly We Who have revealed the Reminder, and it is certainly We Who will preserve it."[62] No one can change, alter or distort its meanings and no one can add or delete anything from the Quran. If someone were to try to do so, then they would find no one to help them or protect them. "And you will never find refuge other than with Him." True safety, refuge, protection, and security rests with Allah ﷻ alone. This is the first instruction found in this passage; to recite the Quran and act upon it.

Next, Allah ﷻ reminds the Prophet ﷺ to stay in the company of those who are sincere and have faith despite their socio-economic status.

وَاصْبِرْ نَفْسَكَ مَعَ الَّذِينَ يَدْعُونَ رَبَّهُم بِالْغَدَاةِ وَالْعَشِيِّ يُرِيدُونَ
وَجْهَهُ ۖ وَلَا تَعْدُ عَيْنَاكَ عَنْهُمْ تُرِيدُ زِينَةَ الْحَيَاةِ الدُّنْيَا ۖ وَلَا تُطِعْ
مَنْ أَغْفَلْنَا قَلْبَهُ عَن ذِكْرِنَا وَاتَّبَعَ هَوَاهُ وَكَانَ أَمْرُهُ فُرُطًا ﴿٢٨﴾

62 15:9 إِنَّا نَحْنُ نَزَّلْنَا الذِّكْرَ وَإِنَّا لَهُ لَحَافِظُونَ

> 28 Keep yourself content with those who call their Lord morning and evening, seeking His pleasure, and let not your eyes overlook them, seeking the splendor of the worldly life. And do not obey the one whose heart We have made heedless of Our remembrance, and who has followed his desire and whose behavior has exceeded the limits.

This verse has a specific background or context in which it was revealed. One day Uyaynah, one of the chiefs of Makkah, came to the Prophet ﷺ while he was sitting with some of the less well-to-do Muslims. One of them was Salmān al-Fārisī رضي الله عنه, who was wearing clothes made of wool and a turban filled with sweat. Others among the poorer companions were luminaries like Bilāl, Ṣuhaib, ʻAmmār, Khabbāb, and ibn Mas'ūd رضي الله عنهم. ʻUyaynah, being arrogant and prideful because of his wealth and status asked the Prophet ﷺ, "Aren't you bothered by their smell? We are the leaders of Makkah. If we accept Islam then people will follow and accept as well. The only thing preventing us from following you is your closeness to these people. Leave them so we can follow you, or at least make separate gatherings for us." In response, Allah ﷻ revealed this verse, telling the Prophet ﷺ not to follow the advice of the rich leaders of Makkah.[63] Don't pay attention to what they're saying and don't be influenced by their idea or suggestion.

"Keep yourself content with those who call their Lord morning and evening, seeking His pleasure." Meaning, keep the company of those who remember Allah ﷻ, praise Him, glorify Him, and ask only Him day and night regardless of whether they are rich or poor. Their only intention is to seek and earn the pleasure of Allah ﷻ. Allah ﷻ then further emphasizes this point by telling the Prophet ﷺ, "and let not your eyes overlook them, seeking the splendor of the worldly life." Meaning, don't look towards others for help and support besides them. Don't seek to replace them with people who have wealth and status. The Prophet ﷺ wanted ʻUyaynah and the leaders of Quraysh to accept Islam so that the others would follow them. But Allah ﷻ is reminding him that their acceptance or rejection won't affect the cause. Although outwardly it may seem like the rich and wealthy accepting Islam would strengthen the cause, in reality there's no need for them. True strength

63 ibn Kathīr, *Tafsīr al-Quran al-ʻAẓīm*, 9:127

comes from the strength of the faith of your followers; not from material means.

Allah ﷻ then further emphasizes this point by saying, "And do not obey the one whose heart We have made heedless of Our remembrance, and who has followed his desire and whose behavior has exceeded the limits." Don't pay attention to those people who are heedless and lost, who have preferred this world over the life of the Hereafter. Their hearts have become hard and enveloped in darkness that prevents them from seeing and understanding the truth, veiling them from the remembrance of Allah ﷻ. As a result, they follow their desires and exceed all the limits and boundaries set by Allah ﷻ falling into sin and disobedience. This is a very comprehensive description of those people who exceed the limits of Allah ﷻ. Meaning, exceeding the limits set by Allah ﷻ is the end result. It starts with heedlessness, which turns into following desires, which then results in disobeying Allah ﷻ.

One of the most important lessons derived from this reminder is that Islam is the religion of equality. It doesn't differentiate between rich and poor, powerful and weak, educated and uneducated, with respect to their standing before Allah ﷻ. Everybody is equally held accountable and responsible in the sight of Allah ﷻ. Islam places all human beings on the same level in front of God. Within the framework of Islam, no human being is intrinsically better than another. Nobility and being beloved to Allah ﷻ are based on internal factors such as faith, taqwā, sincerity, and righteous deeds. Dignity, honor, status, and nobility are not related to material factors. They have nothing to do with a person's race, ethnicity, language, wealth, nationality, lineage, tribe, caste, education, social status, or skin color. All these are transient. Nobility, dignity, status, and honor come from a person's relationship with Allah ﷻ. "In God's eyes, the most honored of you are the ones most mindful of Him."[64] Similarly, the Prophet ﷺ said, "Truly Allah doesn't look at your appearances or your wealth. Rather He looks at your hearts and your actions."[65] Another narration mentions that as soon as this verse was revealed, the Prophet ﷺ stood up looking for the companions referred to in this verse. He found them at the back of the Masjid busy in the remembrance of Allah ﷻ. When he found them he said, "All praise is for Allah, who has not taken

64 49:13 إِنَّ أَكْرَمَكُمْ عِندَ اللَّهِ أَتْقَاكُمْ

65 Muslim, *k.al-birr wa al-ṣilah wa al-ādāb, b. taḥrīm ẓulm al-muslim wa khadhlihi wa iḥtiqārihi wa damihi wa ʿirḍihi wa mālihi,* 2564

my life until he commanded me to remain content with men from my nation. With them is life and with them is death."[66]

Throughout the Prophetic tradition, we find narrations that encourage us to honor and respect the weak and poor; to treat them with kindness, compassion, sympathy, and generosity. Also, to spend time with them and interact with them. As a matter of fact, Imām al-Nawawī ﷺ in his famous collection of ḥadīth, Riyāḍ al-Ṣāliḥīn (Gardens of the Righteous), has two entire chapters dedicated to this subject. For example, Abū al-Dardā'a ﷺ said, "I heard the Messenger of Allah ﷺ say, 'Seek me among the poor and weak. Truly, you are given victory and provided for on account of the poor and weak among you."[67] The Prophet ﷺ didn't just honor the weak and poor, he loved them and wanted to be among them. He used to supplicate: "O Allah! I ask You for the means to do good, to avoid evil, and to love the poor, and I beseech You to forgive me and have mercy on me."[68]

Our beloved Prophet ﷺ lived by his values. He was given the choice to live a life of ease and comfort or the life of hardship and difficulty. And the Prophet ﷺ chose a life of hardship and difficulty; a life of extreme simplicity. His simplicity is awe-inspiring. Whoever reads about the lifestyle of the Prophet ﷺ, can't help but be moved and have their hearts softened. His wife, Ā'isha ﷺ narrated that after he made this choice, the Prophet ﷺ never ate while reclining, saying: "I eat like a servant eats and I sit like a servant sits." [69]We know that he could have lived the life of a millionaire, but rather he was more generous than the free blowing wind.

Next, Allah ﷻ directs the Prophet ﷺ to declare that the truth has come from Allah and that it is absolutely clear.

66 Wāḥidī, *Asbāb al-Nuzūl*, 306-307

67 Abū Dāwūd, *k. al-jihād, b. fī al-intiṣār bī radhl al-khayl wa al-ḍaʿafah*, 2594

68 Tirmidhī, *k. tafsīr al-quran ʿan rasūl Allah*, 3233

69 Ibn Sad, *tabaqāt al-kubrā*, 902

VERSE 29

وَقُلِ الْحَقُّ مِن رَّبِّكُمْ ۖ فَمَن شَاءَ فَلْيُؤْمِن وَمَن شَاءَ فَلْيَكْفُرْ ۚ
إِنَّا أَعْتَدْنَا لِلظَّالِمِينَ نَارًا أَحَاطَ بِهِمْ سُرَادِقُهَا ۚ وَإِن يَسْتَغِيثُوا
يُغَاثُوا بِمَاءٍ كَالْمُهْلِ يَشْوِي الْوُجُوهَ ۚ بِئْسَ الشَّرَابُ وَسَاءَتْ
مُرْتَفَقًا ﴿٢٩﴾

29 And say, "The truth is from your Lord. Now, whoever so wills may believe and whoever so wills may deny." Verily We have prepared for the wrongdoers a Fire whose canopies will encompass them. And if they will beg for help, they shall be helped with water like molten lead that will scald the faces. Vile is the drink, and how evil a resting place.

In the first part of this verse, Allah ﷻ tells His messenger ﷺ to announce that the truth has come from Him and that it is absolutely clear and straightforward. "And say, 'The truth is from your Lord. Now, whoever so wills may believe and whoever so wills may deny.'" Meaning, O Muḥammad ﷺ! Tell the people that what you are preaching and calling them towards is the absolute truth from your Lord; there is no doubt about it whatsoever. This truth, Islam, is the best way of life that guarantess success in this world and the next. Once a person learns of this truth, they can choose to accept it and believe in it or they can choose to reject it and not to believe in it. Everybody will be held accountable for their own decisions on the Day of Judgment. Some of the commentators mention that this verse was also revealed in connection to the previous incident.

The statement, "Now, whoever so wills may believe and whoever so wills may deny," is meant as a severe warning. The Prophet's ﷺ responsibility is simply to convey the message. Once the message has been conveyed, he's no longer responsible. The individual who receives the message must make the conscious decision to either accept or reject the truth. And whatever they choose to do, they will bear the responsibility of their choice.

The last part of the verse that describes some of the unimaginable torments of hell shows that the first part is meant to be a warning. "Surely, We have prepared for the wrongdoers a fire whose canopies will encompass them. And if they will beg for help, they shall be helped with water like molten lead that will scald the faces. Vile is the drink, and how evil a resting place." The fire of Hell is described as taking the form of canopies that will surround them. They will be surrounded by fire, flames and smoke, on all sides, above and below. The Prophet ﷺ said, "The canopies of hell will have four thick walls and each wall will be equivalent (in size) to the distance of forty years."[70] Allah ﷻ continues describing the horrors of hell saying, "And if they will beg for help, they shall be helped with water like molten lead that will scald the faces. Vile is the drink, and how evil a resting place." When they beg for any sort of help and relief they will be met with more punishment and torture by being given unimaginably boiling hot water. Allah ﷻ likens it to molten lead that is so hot that it causes their skin to melt. Regarding the water of Hellfire that is similar to molten lead, the Prophet ﷺ said, "Like boiling oil, such that when it is brought close to his face, the skin of his face will fall off into it."[71] ibn Abbās رضي الله عنه said, "al-Muhl is thick water similar to oil."[72] Mujāhid رحمه الله mentions that it is made of puss and blood.[73] It is an extremely vile, disgusting, and terrible drink and Hell is the absolute worst place. May Allah ﷻ protect us from the punishment of the hereafter!

Then Allah ﷻ describes His promise of reward to those who believe. This is part of the unique style of the Quran of al-tarhīb (instilling fear) and al-targhīb (instilling hope). Throughout the Quran, whenever Allah ﷻ mentions the non-believers and their punishment He follows it up with a description

70 Tirmidhī, *k. ṣifah jahannam ʿan rasūl Allah*, 2786

71 Tirmidhī, *k. ṣifah jahannam ʿan rasūl Allah*, 2581

72 Qurṭubī, *al-Jamiʿ fī Aḥkām al-Quran*, 13:262

73 Qurṭubī, *al-Jāmiʿ fī Aḥkām al-Quran*, 13:262

of the believers and their reward. This is designed to create a sense of both fear and hope. When we recite verses describing punishment and reflect upon them, it creates a feeling of fear; we fear the Day of Judgment, standing in front of Allah ﷻ, being held accountable, and punishment. When we recite verses describing reward and reflect upon them, it creates a sense of hope in Allah's infinite mercy, forgiveness, grace, bounty, and reward.

إِنَّ الَّذِينَ آمَنُوا وَعَمِلُوا الصَّالِحَاتِ إِنَّا لَا نُضِيعُ أَجْرَ مَنْ أَحْسَنَ
عَمَلًا ﴿٣٠﴾ أُولَٰئِكَ لَهُمْ جَنَّاتُ عَدْنٍ تَجْرِي مِن تَحْتِهِمُ الْأَنْهَارُ
يُحَلَّوْنَ فِيهَا مِنْ أَسَاوِرَ مِن ذَهَبٍ وَيَلْبَسُونَ ثِيَابًا خُضْرًا
مِّن سُندُسٍ وَإِسْتَبْرَقٍ مُّتَّكِئِينَ فِيهَا عَلَى الْأَرَائِكِ ۚ نِعْمَ الثَّوَابُ
وَحَسُنَتْ مُرْتَفَقًا ﴿٣١﴾

[30] As for those who believe and do righteous deeds, -of course, We do not waste the reward of those who are good in deeds. [31] Those are the ones for whom there are eternal gardens, rivers flowing beneath them. They will be adorned therein with bracelets of gold, and they will be dressed in green garments, made of fine silk and thick silk, reclining therein on couches. Excellent is the reward and beautiful is Paradise as a resting-place."

In these verses, Allah ﷻ is describing His promise to the righteous and fortunate believers who try their best to practice their faith and remain steadfast upon it. "Truly those who believe and do righteous deeds, -of course, We do not waste the reward of those who are good in deeds." Faith, īmān, and righteous deeds are always mentioned together; they are inseparable. This is the simple formula for success both in this world and the next. Our faith, our īmān, has to be something that's real and active; something that translates into action. Once it fills our hearts, it expresses itself through our speech and behavior. Faith is the catalyst behind our thoughts, attitudes, morals, values, principles, and guides how we live our lives. It is this faith coupled with righteous deeds that will allow us to earn the mercy of Allah ﷻ. Allah ﷻ, through His infinite mercy and grace, will definitely reward us for our good deeds.

Allah ﷻ then describes some of the rewards and luxuries waiting for us in the life of the hereafter. He ﷻ mentions four specific things:

1. "Those are the ones for whom there are eternal gardens, rivers flowing beneath them." They will be given eternal gardens beneath which rivers flow residing in palaces for all of eternity. Paradise is described as a "sparkling light, aromatic plants, a lofty palace, a flowing river, ripe fruit, a beautiful wife and abundant clothing, in an eternal abode of radiant joy, in beautiful, soundly-constructed high houses."[74]

2. "They will be adorned therein with bracelets of gold." The people of paradise will be wearing bracelets of gold, silver, and pearls. The beauty and elegance of these bracelets is beyond human imagination.

3. "They will be dressed in green garments, made of fine silk and thick silk." They will be wearing these extremely beautiful green-colored clothes made of fine silk. Allah ﷻ describes the silk garments of Paradise in several verses throughout the Quran. al-Barā' ibn Āzib ؓ narrates that a silk garment was brought to the Messenger of Allah ﷺ, which the Companions began to admire because of its beauty and softness. The Prophet ﷺ said, "The handkerchiefs of Sad ibn Muādh in Paradise are better than this."[75]

4. "Reclining therein on couches." They will be relaxing and reclining on couches in the ultimate state of comfort, pleasure, and enjoyment.

Syed Quṭb ؒ remarks, "Gold jewelry, fine silk garments and raised

---

74 ibn Mājah, *k. al-zuhd, b. ṣifāt al-jannah*, 4332

75 Bukhārī, *k. bad' al-khalq, b. mā jā'a fī ṣifāt al-jannah wa al-nār*,

couches would all have signified immense luxury, particularly in the context of Arabian desert life, where rough woolen garments and sitting on the ground were the norm."[76] How beautiful and amazing is the reward of Paradise and what an amazing place it is. May Allah ﷻ make us all among the inhabitants of Paradise!

KEY LESSONS FROM VERSES 27-31

1.

Reciting the Quran on a consistent and regular basis and trying one's best to follow its guidance - This is a responsibility upon each and every single Muslim. We should strive to establish and develop a real and intimate relationship with the Quran. It is essential for every single one of us to nurture, develop, and build a relationship with the Quran by reciting it regularly, reflecting and pondering over its meanings, and implementing its teachings and guidance into our daily lives.

2.

The Divine preservation and protection of the Quran - Allah ﷻ has taken the responsibility of protecting and preserving the Quran; it is divinely protected.

3.

Keeping good company - Whether we recognize it or not, our environment has a very powerful impact upon our lives. It affects our mindset, attitude, speech, and behavior. The Prophet ﷺ told us, "A person is upon the way of life of their close friend, so be careful who you choose as a close friend."[77]

---

76 Quṭb, *fī Ẓilāl al-Quran*,

77 Tirmidhī, *k. al-zuhd*, 2378

4.

Real equality - Islam establishes real and true equality between all people. Equality in Islam is not seen through the lens of material qualties or attributes of an individual confined to the limits of the present world. Equality in Islam transcends the material and gives consideration to the equality of souls in front of God.

5.

Islam is the absolute truth - Islam, total and complete submission to Allah ﷻ both internally and externally is the only truth. It is the only path to achieve success in this world and salvation in the life to come.

6.

Punishment for disbelief - Allah ﷻ, if He so wills, will hold people accountable in the life of the hereafter for their sins and rejection of the truth according to His infinite and divine justice.

7.

Reward for belief - Allah ﷻ will reward those who believe and do righteous deeds through His infinite and divine mercy and grace.

The next set of verses, verses 32-44, discuss the story of two people, a rich man who was fooled by his wealth and a poor man who was honored for his conviction and belief, and the conversation they had with one another. In this set of verses Allah ﷻ has given us an example of a rich non-believer who was fooled by his wealth, and a poor believer who was guided through his belief. Through this example Allah ﷻ shows us that wealth isn't the true source of pride or honor; rather belief and obedience of Allah ﷻ brings real pride, honor, and respect. The first man thinks he's extremely powerful because of the wealth he has and that causes him to forget about the Supreme Power who controls everything in a person's life. The other is a believer who values his faith. He always remembers Allah ﷻ, realizing that the blessings he has are a gift from Him. He recognizes the importance of praising Allah ﷻ and gratitude.

There is a discussion among the scholars of the Quran regarding the identity of these two individuals. There are a few different reports. One mentions that they were two brothers from the people of Makkah from the tribe of Banū Makhzūm.[78] According to ibn 'Abbās ؓ they were two brothers from Bani Israel; one was a believer, the other a non-believer. They inherited 8,000 dinars (gold coins) from their father that they split in half. The non-believer bought land, gardens, and invested his wealth. The believer spent his money in charity. The story goes that the non-believing brother purchased some land for 1,000 dirhams (silver coins). In response, the believing brother said, "O Allah so and so purchased land for 1,000 dirhams and I'm purchas-

78 Qurṭubī, *al-Jāmiʿ fī Aḥkām al-Quran*, 13:269

ing land from you in Paradise for 1,000 dirhams." He gave 1,000 in charity. The same thing happened with respect to building a house, marriage, servants, and possessions. Each time one brother spent money on something the other donated an equal amount in charity. One spent all of his money on material things and invested it, while the other gave all of his money away in charity hoping for reward from Allah ﷻ. The one who invested his money became extremely wealthy while the believing brother was then afflicted with severe need and poverty.[79]

وَاضْرِبْ لَهُم مَّثَلًا رَّجُلَيْنِ جَعَلْنَا لِأَحَدِهِمَا جَنَّتَيْنِ مِنْ أَعْنَابٍ
وَحَفَفْنَاهُمَا بِنَخْلٍ وَجَعَلْنَا بَيْنَهُمَا زَرْعًا ﴿٣٢﴾ كِلْتَا الْجَنَّتَيْنِ آتَتْ
أُكُلَهَا وَلَمْ تَظْلِم مِّنْهُ شَيْئًا ۚ وَفَجَّرْنَا خِلَالَهُمَا نَهَرًا ﴿٣٣﴾

[32] Give them an example (the parable) of two men. We gave one of them two gardens of grapevines, and surrounded both of them with date palms, and placed crops between them. [33] Both the gardens brought forth their fruit, and suppressed nothing from it, and We caused a stream to flow through them."

Allah ﷻ is telling His Prophet ﷺ to give this example, this parable, of two men to the rich and powerful of Makkah and those similar to them who refused to accept his message. This is an example

79 Qurṭubī, *al-Jāmiʿ fī Aḥkām al-Quran*, 13:271

and reminder for anyone who is attached to the material world and has adopted a materialistic mindset. The example starts by describing the wealth of the non-believer. "We gave one of them two gardens of grapevines, and surrounded both of them with date palms, and placed crops between them. Both the gardens brought forth their fruit, and suppressed nothing from it, and We caused a stream to flow through them." He was given two beautiful gardens filled with grape vines. Both of these gardens were surrounded by date palms and in between these gardens were farms. There were also streams flowing through these gardens. This land was extremely fertile so the gardens, farms, and date palms produced a lot of fruit and produce. Not only did he own this beautiful land and these amazing gardens and farms, he was also given a lot of other material wealth.

VERSE 34

وَكَانَ لَهُۥ ثَمَرٌ فَقَالَ لِصَٰحِبِهِۦ وَهُوَ يُحَاوِرُهُۥٓ أَنَا۠ أَكۡثَرُ مِنكَ مَالٗا وَأَعَزُّ نَفَرٗا ﴿٣٤﴾

[34] And he had [abundant] fruit (wealth) So, he said to his companion while conversing with him, "I am greater than you in wealth and stronger in manpower."

"And he had wealth." According to ibn Abbās ﵄, this is referring to gold, silver, and other material wealth.[80] All of this wealth, all of these material goods caused him to become arrogant, haughty, conceited, and full of pride. He was fooled and deceived by his wealth,

80 Qurṭubī, *al-Jāmiʿ fī Aḥkām al-Quran*, 13:275

just as we see so many rich and powerful people fooled by their wealth. According to one of the narratives mentioned in Qurṭubī,[81] when his brother fell on hard times, he approached his wealthy brother expecting some sort of goodness. However, his brother's heart had become hard and corrupt from his love for the material. He responded to his brother's request by showing off his wealth saying, "I am greater than you in wealth and stronger in manpower." Full of arrogance and pride, he told his brother that I'm more well off than you and I have more servants, workers, and children than you. His arrogance, pride and wealth blinded him to such an extent that he became extremely ungrateful and heedless. His love for this material world blinded him to such an extent that it led him to denying the finite nature of this world and the reality of the Day of Judgment.

VERSES 35-36

وَدَخَلَ جَنَّتَهُۥ وَهُوَ ظَالِمٌ لِّنَفْسِهِۦ قَالَ مَآ أَظُنُّ أَن تَبِيدَ هَٰذِهِۦٓ
أَبَدًا ﴿٣٥﴾ وَمَآ أَظُنُّ ٱلسَّاعَةَ قَآئِمَةً وَلَئِن رُّدِدتُّ إِلَىٰ رَبِّى لَأَجِدَنَّ خَيْرًا
مِّنْهَا مُنقَلَبًا ﴿٣٦﴾

35 And he entered his garden while he was doing wrong to himself. He said, "I do not think that this will ever perish,
36 and I do not think that the Hour (Day of Judgment) will come. And even if I am sent back to my Lord, I will surely find a better place than this to resort to."

81 Qurṭubī, *al-Jāmiʿ fī Aḥkām al-Quran*, 13:271

In these verses, Allah ﷻ is describing the scene to us to make it more real and relatable. This man entered one of his gardens while conversing with his brother. He was talking about his wealth and material possessions and looking down upon and belittling his brother. He is described as "wronging himself" because of his disbelief, arrogance, and denial of resurrection. He primarily wronged himself through his ingratitude; his pride and refusal to acknowledge that his provision, wealth, properties, gardens, and children are a gift and blessing from Allah ﷻ. The abundance of his material possessions fooled, tricked, and deceived him into believing that they will never perish. "I don't think that any of this will perish." All of these things that I have, these gardens, crops, gold, silver, servants, children, and property will last forever. He became heedless and neglectful of the impermanence of all created things and his own mortality. "I don't believe that there is a Day of Judgment." His materialism led him to denying life after death.

One of the reasons why he is described as wronging himself is because he should have been thanking Allah ﷻ for all of these blessings, but instead he was ungrateful. Instead of adopting an attitude of humility and gratitude, he adopted an attitude of arrogance and ungratefulness. He thought that all of these material blessings were a sign that his Lord must be pleased with him. If He weren't, then He would not have blessed him with so many favors. He falsely believed that having wealth and power was a sign of being honored and having a high station in the sight of Allah ﷻ. If there were a Day of Judgment or a Hereafter, then he assumes that he would be given more there than he was given here in the world. "And even if I am sent back to my Lord, I will surely find a better place than this to resort to." Again, he doesn't believe in life after death. He is saying that hypothetically speaking if there were a life after death, then he would be blessed there as well, just as he was blessed here in the life of this world. Allah ﷻ then tells us how his believing brother - recognizing the ignorance, shallowness and ridiculousness of his argument - responded to him.

قَالَ لَهُۥ صَاحِبُهُۥ وَهُوَ يُحَاوِرُهُۥٓ أَكَفَرْتَ بِٱلَّذِى خَلَقَكَ مِن تُرَابٍ
ثُمَّ مِن نُّطْفَةٍ ثُمَّ سَوَّىٰكَ رَجُلًا ﴿٣٧﴾ لَّٰكِنَّا۠ هُوَ ٱللَّهُ رَبِّى وَلَآ أُشْرِكُ
بِرَبِّىٓ أَحَدًا ﴿٣٨﴾

[37] His companion said to him as he conversed with him, "Do you deny the One who created you from dust, then from a drop (of semen), then fashioned you as a man? [38] But He is Allah, my Lord, and I do not associate anyone with my Lord.

This is a very beautiful response given by the less well-to-do brother. While having this conversation, he responds to him asking him in astonishment and amazement, "Do you really deny the One who created you from dust, then a drop of reproductive fluid, and then fashioned you as a man?" This question is meant as a mawiẓah, a reminder or a heart softener; something that's supposed to move the heart of his brother and appeal to his heart and mind. How in the world can you deny the existence of the One who is the source of all your wealth, the One who gave you these amazing blessings, the One who brought you into existence? He also declares his firm belief and commitment to Allah ﷻ. "But He is Allah, my Lord, and I do not associate anyone with my Lord." He acknowledges, recognizes, and believes with absolute certainty that Allah ﷻ is his Lord. The only Being worthy and deserving of worship, servitude, submission, and obedience. He continues advising and counseling his brother reminding him how his attitude should be towards all of these blessings. The attitude of faith, submission, recognition, and obedience.

VERSES 39-41

وَلَوْلَآ إِذْ دَخَلْتَ جَنَّتَكَ قُلْتَ مَا شَآءَ ٱللَّهُ لَا قُوَّةَ إِلَّا بِٱللَّهِ ۚ إِن
تَرَنِ أَنَا۠ أَقَلَّ مِنكَ مَالًا وَوَلَدًا ﴿٣٩﴾ فَعَسَىٰ رَبِّىٓ أَن يُؤْتِيَنِ خَيْرًا
مِّن جَنَّتِكَ وَيُرْسِلَ عَلَيْهَا حُسْبَانًا مِّنَ ٱلسَّمَآءِ فَتُصْبِحَ صَعِيدًا
زَلَقًا ﴿٤٠﴾ أَوْ يُصْبِحَ مَآؤُهَا غَوْرًا فَلَن تَسْتَطِيعَ لَهُۥ طَلَبًا ﴿٤١﴾

[39] If only, when you had entered your garden, you had said, 'This is what Allah has willed. There is no power except with Allah.' If you see that I am less than you in wealth and children, [40] it may be that my Lord will give me something better than your garden, and unleash against it a reckoning from the sky, so that it becomes barren land. [41] Or its water may sink deep, so that you cannot seek after it.

He's telling his brother that instead of being full of pride, boastful, conceited, and arrogant, he should've been grateful, thankful, humble, and appreciative to Allah ﷻ. He should've thanked and praised Allah ﷻ by saying, "This is what Allah has willed. There is no power except with Allah." Meaning, whatever happens in this world happens according to the will and decree of Allah ﷻ. This is an expression of gratitude and humility. By saying this, he would have shown thanks to Allah ﷻ for his wealth, children, and properties and at the same time would be recognizing that all of it is from Allah ﷻ. These are two very important phrases that we as Muslims are encouraged to learn and say often. Anytime we see something that we like or think is beautiful and amazing we should say, "This is what Allah has willed. There is no power except with Allah." This is a very common phrase in our everyday speech and it indicates a recognition that nothing happens outside of the will of Allah ﷻ.

"There is no power except with Allah" is also a common phrase that we use, which acknowledges that we can't achieve or do anything without the help of Allah ﷻ. It's also used when we feel helpless in the face of some difficulty or hardship. It's also considered to be a treasure from the treasures of Paradise. Abū Mūsa ؓ narrated that the Prophet ﷺ said to him, "Shall I not direct you to a treasure from the treasures of Paradise? It's to say there is no power or strength except with Allah."[82] Ibn Kathīr ؒ mentions that this verse is the source of our practice and custom of saying "As Allah wills" whenever we are pleased with something.[83] Anas ؓ narrated that the Prophet ﷺ said, "Whoever sees something they like should say, 'As Allah wills, there is no strength except with Allah' and it will not be affected by the evil eye."[84]

There are several narrations from the Prophet ﷺ that mention the virtues, blessings, and rewards associated with mentioning the name of Allah ﷻ and His power. Anas ؓ narrates that the Prophet ﷺ said, "When a man goes out of his house and says: 'In the name of Allah, I trust in Allah; there is no might and no power but in Allah,' the following will be said to him at that time: 'You are guided, defended, and protected.' The devils will go far from him and another devil will say: 'How can you deal with a man who has been guided, defended and protected?'"[85]

After counseling and explaining to his more well-off brother what the right attitude should be towards wealth, material possessions, and blessings he responds to his boasts and claims saying, "If you see that I am less than you in wealth and children, it may be that my Lord will give me something better than your garden." He tells him that if you consider me to be less well off than you in this world, in terms of wealth and children, then I hope that my situation will be different in the Hereafter because of my sincerity and

---

82 Muslim, *k. al-dhikr wa al-duʿā wa al-tawbah wa al-istighfār, b. istiḥbāb khafḍ al-ṣawt bi al-dhikr*, 2704

83 ibn Kathīr, *Tafsīr al-Quran al-ʿAẓīm*, 9:138

84 Qurṭubī, *al-Jāmiʿ fī Aḥkām al-Quran*, 13:282

85 Abū Dāwūd, *k. al-adab, b. Mā yaqūlu al-rajul idhā kharaja min baytihi*, 5095

faith. He believes that Allah ﷻ will reward him with something much better than the gardens of his brother in the life to come because of his faith and humility. He then warns him of the transient and temporary nature of the life of this world; that one day you could have all of these amazing and wonderful things and the next day it could be gone literally within the blink of an eye. "And unleash against it a reckoning from the sky, so that it becomes a flattened plain. Or its water may sink deep, so that you cannot seek after it." It's possible that some sort of calamity, torrential rains, a storm, or any other natural disaster can come from the sky and completely destroy the gardens leaving it without any growth or vegetation. The land will become a "flattened plain" barren and dead. It's possible that the water from the springs will sink deep into the earth and you won't be able to access it leaving your gardens to slowly wither and die.

Syed Quṭb رحمه الله while commenting on these verses writes, "This is an example of how faith makes a believer very powerful. He does not care for wealth, might, or arrogance. He states the truth clearly, without hesitation, or cowardice. There is no room for bending the truth in order to please anyone, be that a friend or someone mighty. A believer feels that he is far higher than all power and wealth. What God has for him is far superior to any riches or pleasures this life may bring. God's grace is all that he seeks, and His grace is plentiful and always available. On the other hand, God's punishment is severe and could befall the arrogant at any time."[86]

The Sūrah then tells us that the warning of his brother actually came true. Allah ﷻ sent down some type of punishment, a storm or something else, that completely destroyed all of his wealth and belongings.

86 Quṭb, *fī Ẓilāl al-Quran*, 4:2271

VERSE 42

وَأُحِيطَ بِثَمَرِهِۦ فَأَصْبَحَ يُقَلِّبُ كَفَّيْهِ عَلَىٰ مَآ أَنفَقَ فِيهَا وَهِىَ
خَاوِيَةٌ عَلَىٰ عُرُوشِهَا وَيَقُولُ يَٰلَيْتَنِى لَمْ أُشْرِكْ بِرَبِّىٓ أَحَدًا ﴿٤٢﴾

[42] And his fruit was encompassed. So he began to wring his hands on account of what he had spent on it while it lay in waste upon its trellises saying, "I wish I had not associated anyone with my Lord!"

"And his fruit was encompassed," meaning his wealth, property, and gardens were encompassed by ruin; they were completely destroyed. Allah ﷻ describes it as "it lay in waste upon its trellises". When he saw his possessions - his land and gardens - destroyed before his eyes and how he wasn't able to do anything about it, he realized his faults. He began to wring his hands as a sign of remorse, sorrow, anxiety, worry, and regret. He now realized that what his brother said was true and he was repentant for having associated partners with Allah ﷻ. "I wish I had not associated anyone with my Lord!"

The Sūrah concludes this story or example by declaring in all clarity that all protection comes from Allah ﷻ; all power belongs to Him and all support comes from Him. His ﷻ reward is the best reward and what He stores for us is the best and everlasting.

وَلَمْ تَكُن لَّهُۥ فِئَةٌ يَنصُرُونَهُۥ مِن دُونِ ٱللَّهِ وَمَا كَانَ مُنتَصِرًا ﴿٤٣﴾
هُنَالِكَ ٱلْوَلَٰيَةُ لِلَّهِ ٱلْحَقِّ ۚ هُوَ خَيْرٌ ثَوَابًا وَخَيْرٌ عُقْبًا ﴿٤٤﴾

[33] And he had no forces to help him other than Allah; nor could he help himself. [34] In that situation, protection belongs to Allah, the True God. He is best in reward and best in requital.

Despite his pride, arrogance, and claims of power and strength, at this time of loss and destruction, he finds himself absolutely humbled and helpless. There's no group, party, or children to help him except for Allah ﷻ. He couldn't even help himself. It's at that specific moment that he realized that all protection and power comes from Allah ﷻ alone; all might, power, authority, support, and decision making belong to Him alone. "In that situation, protection belongs to Allah, the True God." Allah alone is the Walī, the Protector and Guardian and He is the Truth. "He is best in reward and best in requital." He ﷻ gives the best reward both in this world and the next. People should place their hopes in the everlasting and unimaginable rewards granted by Allah ﷻ, not the temporary and finite rewards of this material world.

This story is a clear reminder of the difference between true belief and disbelief. A true believer is concerned about the life to come and the disbeliever is consumed with the life of this world. This story is a powerful reminder of the reality of the life of this world. Through this story, we're reminded that the life of this world is temporary and fleeting; that, you and I, we're not going to be here forever. The world will eventually come to an end.

And that the life to come, the life of the hereafter, is a life of eternity.

This is a message that is echoed and emphasized in several places throughout the Quran. Allah ﷻ says:

1. "O my people, this worldly life is only [temporary] enjoyment, and indeed, the Hereafter - that is the home of [permanent] settlement."[87]
2. "Say, The enjoyment of this world is little, and the Hereafter is better for he who fears Allah."[88]
3. "But you prefer the worldly life, while the Hereafter is better and more enduring."[89]

The Quran constantly reminds us not to be fooled, tricked and deceived by the life of this world.

4. "And what is the life of this world except the enjoyment of delusion?"[90]
5. "O mankind, indeed the promise of Allah is truth, so let not the worldly life delude you and be not deceived about Allah by the Deceiver."[91]

One of the most consuming and powerful diseases of the heart is love of the world. The Prophet ﷺ told us, "Love of the world is the origin of every sin."[92] The Prophet ﷺ also told us, "The life of the world is sweet and green. Allah makes you generations succeeding one another, so that He may try you in respect of your actions. So beware of the beguilements of the world and those of women. The first trial of the Children of Israel was through women."[93]

---

87 40:39 يَا قَوْمِ إِنَّمَا هَـٰذِهِ الْحَيَاةُ الدُّنْيَا مَتَاعٌ وَإِنَّ الْآخِرَةَ هِيَ دَارُ الْقَرَارِ

88 4:77 قُلْ مَتَاعُ الدُّنْيَا قَلِيلٌ وَالْآخِرَةُ خَيْرٌ لِّمَنِ اتَّقَىٰ

89 87:16-17 بَلْ تُؤْثِرُونَ الْحَيَاةَ الدُّنْيَا * وَالْآخِرَةُ خَيْرٌ وَأَبْقَىٰ

90 3:185 وَمَا الْحَيَاةُ الدُّنْيَا إِلَّا مَتَاعُ الْغُرُورِ

91 35:5 يَا أَيُّهَا النَّاسُ إِنَّ وَعْدَ اللَّـهِ حَقٌّ ۖ فَلَا تَغُرَّنَّكُمُ الْحَيَاةُ الدُّنْيَا ۖ وَلَا يَغُرَّنَّكُم بِاللَّـهِ الْغَرُورُ

92 al-Suyūṭī, *Tadrīb al-Rāwī*, 1:486

93 Muslim, *k. al-Riqāq, b. akthar ahl al-jannah al-fuqarā'a wa akthar ahl al-nār al-nisā'a wa bayān al-fitnah bī al-nisā'a*, 2742

KEY LESSONS FROM THE STORY OF THE OWNER OF TWO GARDENS

1.

The dangers and harms of arrogance, pride, and ingratitude.

2.

The importance of humility and gratitude.

3.

The finite and temporary nature of this world, as opposed to the infinite and everlasting nature of the world to come.

4.

Love of the world blinds a person from seeing the truth.

5.

All blessings are gifts from Allah ﷻ.

6.

Everything happens according to the divine will, decree, and wisdom of Allah ﷻ.

7.

True wealth is in contentment, not material things.

8.

Faith and materialism are in conflict with each other.

9.

Wealth can be taken away in the blink of an eye.

10.

There's no true guardian or protector other than Allah ﷻ.

11.

Mankind is weak and helpless without Allah ﷻ.

In the next few verses, Allah ﷻ discusses a few different topics. Verses 45-46 give us an example of the temporary nature of this world. Verses 47-49 describe some of the events that will take place on the Day of Judgment. Verses 50-53 discuss the story of Adam and Satan. Verses 54-59 discuss a number of topics related to faith and the Quran.

VERSE 45

وَاضْرِبْ لَهُم مَّثَلَ الْحَيَاةِ الدُّنْيَا كَمَاءٍ أَنزَلْنَاهُ مِنَ السَّمَاءِ فَاخْتَلَطَ
بِهِ نَبَاتُ الْأَرْضِ فَأَصْبَحَ هَشِيمًا تَذْرُوهُ الرِّيَاحُ ۗ وَكَانَ اللَّهُ عَلَىٰ كُلِّ
شَيْءٍ مُّقْتَدِرًا ﴿٤٥﴾

[45] Give them the parable (example) of the life of this world: It is like water We send down from the sky. Then it mixes

with the vegetation of the earth. Then it becomes chaff, scattered by the winds. And Allah is capable of all things.

In these verses Allah ﷻ gives us an example of the reality of the life of this world and its temporary and fleeting nature to show us its true value. Allah ﷻ wants us to recognize the real value of this life, especially in comparison to the life to come. We're reminded in a very brief, yet powerful way that the life of this world is temporary and fleeting; that it will very quickly come to an end. This example highlights and emphasizes the main moral from the story of the man with two gardens covered in the previous passage. Similar to the story, these verses are also directed at the rich and powerful members of Quraysh, whose arrogance and pride caused them to look down upon some of the less fortunate Companions of the Prophet ﷺ and anyone with a similar attitude and mindset.

Allah ﷻ tells the Prophet ﷺ to give his community an example of the life of this world. Tell them "It is like water We send down from the sky. Then it mixes with the vegetation of the earth. Then it becomes chaff, scattered by the winds." The fleeting nature of this world is similar to plants and vegetation after they have been watered. Allah ﷻ sends down rain from the sky that causes the earth to turn green; it mixes with the vegetation of the earth giving it life, color, and vibrancy. We're shown a very brief scene of life; the rain causes all these plants to grow. "Then it becomes chaff, scattered by the winds." Chaff is lifeless matter; something that has no real value that is just scattered and blown away by the wind. That's exactly how the life of this world is. At one moment it's vibrant and alive and at the next moment it will be gone. It doesn't last. It has an expiration date. The world is just like a field of green crops, or a beautiful, lush, green garden - something that brings enjoyment, pleasure, and benefit. But none of these things lasts forever. The crops, the plants, trees, and flowers slowly dry, wilt, and start to turn yellow. Then they becomes straw-like and crumble, going from being something beautiful, useful, and pleasing to being something that just blows away in the wind. Allah ﷻ is telling us that's exactly how the world is. These are all the things we work for and invest in throughout our lives. We run after them, but in the end what happens? All of it ceases to exist. It no longer matters.

Imām al-Qurṭubī رحمه الله beautifully describes why the world is compared to water. "Allah ﷻ compares the world to water because water doesn't settle in one place just as the world doesn't remain with one person. Water doesn't remain in one state, just as the world. Water doesn't remain, but evaporates just as the world will cease to exist. No one is able to submerge themselves in water without getting wet, just as one is unable to protect themselves from trials and tribulations by submerging themselves in the world. A particular amount of water is beneficial and causes plants to grow, and if it exceeds that amount it is harmful and destructive, just as the right amount of the world is beneficial, and anything extra is harmful."[94] The Prophet ﷺ said, "He has succeeded who accepts Islam, and is provided with what is sufficient and is made content by Allah."[95]

Every single thing that exists will cease to exist - this entire universe and everything it contains - and the only thing that actually remains is the consequence of our faith. Allah ﷻ ends the verse by reminding us, "And Allah is capable of all things." Meaning He has the power to create and bring things into existence, the power to bring things to an end, and the power to bring them back to life. This example of the life of the world has been given in the Quran in a number of different places. For instance Allah ﷻ says in Sūrah al-Zumar, "Do you not see that Allah sends down rain from the sky—channelling it through streams in the earth—then produces with it crops of various colours, then they dry up and you see them wither, and then He reduces them to chaff? Surely in this is a reminder for people of reason."[96] He ﷻ also says in Sūrah al-Ḥadīd, "Know that this worldly life is no more than play, amusement, luxury, mutual boasting, and competition in wealth and children. This is like rain that causes plants to grow, to the delight of the planters. But later the plants dry up and you see them wither, then they are reduced to chaff. And in the Hereafter there will be either severe punishment or forgiveness and pleasure of Allah, whereas the life of this world is no more than the delusion of enjoyment."[97]

Allah ﷻ then further clarifies this point by telling us what has true, ev-

---

94 Qurṭubī, *al-Jāmiʿ fī Aḥkām al-Quran*, 13:289

95 Tirmidhī, *k. al-zuhd ʿan rasūlillah, b. mā jāʾa fī al-kafāf wa al-ṣabr ʿalayhi*, 2348

96 39:21 أَلَمْ تَرَ أَنَّ اللَّهَ أَنزَلَ مِنَ السَّمَاءِ مَاءً فَسَلَكَهُ يَنَابِيعَ فِي الْأَرْضِ ثُمَّ يُخْرِجُ بِهِ زَرْعًا مُّخْتَلِفًا أَلْوَانُهُ ثُمَّ يَهِيجُ فَتَرَاهُ مُصْفَرًّا ثُمَّ يَجْعَلُهُ حُطَامًا ۚ إِنَّ فِي ذَٰلِكَ لَذِكْرَىٰ لِأُولِي الْأَلْبَابِ

97 57:20 اعْلَمُوا أَنَّمَا الْحَيَاةُ الدُّنْيَا لَعِبٌ وَلَهْوٌ وَزِينَةٌ وَتَفَاخُرٌ بَيْنَكُمْ وَتَكَاثُرٌ فِي الْأَمْوَالِ وَالْأَوْلَادِ ۖ كَمَثَلِ غَيْثٍ أَعْجَبَ الْكُفَّارَ نَبَاتُهُ ثُمَّ يَهِيجُ فَتَرَاهُ مُصْفَرًّا ثُمَّ يَكُونُ حُطَامًا ۖ وَفِي الْآخِرَةِ عَذَابٌ شَدِيدٌ وَمَغْفِرَةٌ مِّنَ اللَّهِ وَرِضْوَانٌ ۚ وَمَا الْحَيَاةُ الدُّنْيَا إِلَّا مَتَاعُ الْغُرُورِ

erlasting value. He does so by contrasting it to what we value most in this world; wealth and children. The contrast between the two is very sharp and is meant to be hard hitting.

الْمَالُ وَالْبَنُونَ زِينَةُ الْحَيَاةِ الدُّنْيَا ۖ وَالْبَاقِيَاتُ الصَّالِحَاتُ خَيْرٌ
عِندَ رَبِّكَ ثَوَابًا وَخَيْرٌ أَمَلًا ﴿٤٦﴾

[46] Wealth and children are the adornment of the life of this world, and the everlasting good deeds are far better with your Lord in reward and in hope.

Wealth and children are two of the most important things that we value in this life; as a matter of fact they're probably the most important things in our lives. If we truly think about it, the vast majority of our time, energy, resources, and thoughts are spent on earning money and taking care of our children. We're constantly worried about our jobs, salaries, savings, expenses, the mortgage, and the car payment. We're continuously thinking about our children's education; what school they'll go to and what profession they'll choose. Allah ﷻ is reminding us that "wealth and children are the adornment of the life of this world."

The word "zīnah" means beauty, adornment, and decoration. Wealth and children have been made attractive and beautiful for us; they capture our attention. Allah ﷻ tells us something similar in Sūrah Āl Imrān, "Made to seem fair unto mankind is the love of passions, among them women, children, hoarded heaps of gold and silver, horses of mark, cattle and tillage.

Those are the enjoyments of the life of this world. And Allah, with Him is the beautiful return."[98] Allah ﷻ also says, "Your wealth and your children are only a test for you. There is great reward with God."[99] Regarding wealth and children, Allah ﷻ also says, "O believers! Indeed, some of your spouses and children are enemies to you, so beware of them."[100] Allah ﷻ describes wealth and children as adornment of the life of this world, a test, and enemies. This only holds true when they become a distraction and interfere with our true purpose in life.

It's important to note that the enjoyments of this world aren't bad in and of themselves. Islam doesn't prevent us from enjoying these things. As a matter of fact, they have been praised elsewhere in the Quran and Ḥadīth. But, it does teach us the correct guidelines and ways in which to enjoy them. They should never take us away or prevent us from fulfilling our true purpose in life, which is to worship Allah ﷻ. And we're reminded that just like anything else in this world, they too will one day cease to exist. So we shouldn't be fooled, deceived, and tricked by them as well. We shouldn't place all of our hopes, expectations, wants, and wishes in the finite.

Rather, we should focus on what is everlasting; those things that will benefit us in this world and more importantly in the next. "And the everlasting good deeds are far better with your Lord in reward and in hope." "The everlasting good deeds" include every single good deed we can think of; whether they're big or small. This includes all acts of worship such as praying, fasting, giving charity, supplication, and dhikr. It includes being kind to our families, our parents, children, relatives, friends, and neighbors. All of these things "are of far greater merit in your Lord's sight, and a far better source of hope" because their consequences are everlasting. Ibn 'Abbās ﷺ mentions that the "everlasting good deeds" are the five daily prayers or any righteous statement or action. He also said they are to say subḥānAllah, alḥamdulillah, lā ilāha illa Allah and Allahu Akbar.[101] Imām Mālik ﷺ records a narration that mentions they are "a slave's saying Allah is greater (Allahu Akbar) and Glory be to Allah (subḥānallah) and Praise be to Allah (al-ḥamd lillah) and

---

98 3:14 زُيِّنَ لِلنَّاسِ حُبُّ الشَّهَوَاتِ مِنَ النِّسَاءِ وَالْبَنِينَ وَالْقَنَاطِيرِ الْمُقَنطَرَةِ مِنَ الذَّهَبِ وَالْفِضَّةِ وَالْخَيْلِ الْمُسَوَّمَةِ وَالْأَنْعَامِ وَالْحَرْثِ ۗ ذَٰلِكَ مَتَاعُ الْحَيَاةِ الدُّنْيَا ۖ وَاللَّهُ عِندَهُ حُسْنُ الْمَآبِ

99 64:15 إِنَّمَا أَمْوَالُكُمْ وَأَوْلَادُكُمْ فِتْنَةٌ ۚ وَاللَّهُ عِندَهُ أَجْرٌ عَظِيمٌ

100 64:12 يَا أَيُّهَا الَّذِينَ آمَنُوا إِنَّ مِنْ أَزْوَاجِكُمْ وَأَوْلَادِكُمْ عَدُوًّا لَّكُمْ فَاحْذَرُوهُمْ

101 Qurṭubī, *al-Jāmiʿ fī Aḥkām al-Quran*, 13:292

There is no god but Allah and there is no power and no strength except by Allah (lā ilāha illa Allah wa la ḥawla wa la quwwatah illa bi Allah)."[102] Abū Saīd al-Khudrī ﷺ narrates that the Prophet ﷺ said, "Increase the everlasting virtues." It was said, "What are they, O Messenger of Allah ﷺ?" He said, "al-Takbīr, al-tahlīl, al-tasbīḥ, al-taḥmīd, and lā ḥawla wa la quwwatah illa bi Allah."[103] Abū Dardā'a ﷺ narrates that the Prophet ﷺ said, "I advise you to say subḥānallah, al-ḥamd lillah, lā ilāha illa Allah, Allahu akbar and lā ḥawla wa lā quwwatah illa billah. They shed sins like a tree sheds its leaves."[104] Anas ﷺ narrates that the Prophet ﷺ passed by a tree with dry leaves, so he struck it with his staff, making the leaves fall. Then he said, "Indeed, all praise is due to Allah, (al-ḥamdulillāh), glory to Allah (subḥān Allah), none has the right to be worshipped but Allah (lā Ilāha Illa Allah), and Allah is the greatest (Allahu akbar) cause the sins to fall from the worshipper, just as the leaves of this tree fall."[105] 'Alī ﷺ said, "Wealth and children are the harvest of the world, and righteous deeds are the harvest of the hereafter. And Allah has gathered both for some people."

All of these things - righteous deeds, statements, acts of worship and obedience - are more valuable than any material possession. And the rationale behind it is simple and straightforward, "And the everlasting good deeds are far better with your Lord in reward and in hope."

al-Qurṭubī ﷺ mentions another very interesting interpretation of "the everlasting good deeds." He brings an opinion from Ubaid ibn Umair ﷺ that it is referring to righteous daughters and the beginning of the verse is an indirect proof of this. Allah ﷻ says, "Wealth and sons are the adornment of the life of this world" and then says "and the everlasting good deeds are far better with your Lord in reward and in hope." Meaning righteous daughters are of far greater merit in Allah's sight for their parents in terms of reward and a far better source of hope in the Hereafter for those who are good to them. Another proof of this is that Ā'ishah ﷺ narrates that, "A woman came to me along with her two daughters. She asked me for (charity) but she found nothing with me except one date, so I gave her that. She accepted it and then divided it between her two daughters and herself ate nothing out of that. She

102 Mālik, *al-Muwaṭṭa*, *k. al-Quran*

103 Aḥmad, *Musnad*, 11731

104 ibn Mājah, *k. al-adab*, *b. faḍl al-tasbīḥ*, 3813

105 Tirmidhī, *k. al-da'wāt 'an rasūlillah*, 3533

then got up and went out, and so did her two daughters. (In the meanwhile) Allah's Messenger ﷺ visited me and I narrated to him her story. Thereupon Allah's Messenger ﷺ said, 'He who is involved (in the responsibility) of (bringing up) daughters, and he accords benevolent treatment towards them, there will be protection for him against Hell-Fire.'"[106] The Prophet ﷺ also said, "Whoever has three daughters and is patient towards them, and feeds them, gives them to drink, and clothes them from his wealth; they will be a shield for him from the Fire on the Day of Resurrection."[107]

The Sūrah now transitions into a brief description of some of the events that will take place on the Day of Judgment; that Day when we'll see the real value of the everlasting deeds.

VERSES 47-48

وَيَوْمَ نُسَيِّرُ الْجِبَالَ وَتَرَى الْأَرْضَ بَارِزَةً وَحَشَرْنَاهُمْ فَلَمْ نُغَادِرْ
مِنْهُمْ أَحَدًا ﴿٤٧﴾ وَعُرِضُوا عَلَىٰ رَبِّكَ صَفًّا لَّقَدْ جِئْتُمُونَا كَمَا
خَلَقْنَاكُمْ أَوَّلَ مَرَّةٍ ۚ بَلْ زَعَمْتُمْ أَلَّن نَّجْعَلَ لَكُم مَّوْعِدًا ﴿٤٨﴾

[47] On the Day We will set the mountains in motion, and you will see the earth as an open plain. And We will gather them, and leave none of them behind. [48] They will be lined up before your Lord in rows. "Indeed you have come to Us as We created you the first time. Nay, but you claimed that We would never appoint a time for you."

106 Muslim, *k. al-birr wa a;-ṣilah wa al-ādāb, b. faḍl al-iḥsān ilā al-banāt*, 2629

107 ibn Mājah, *k. al-adab, b. birr al-wālid wa al-iḥsān ilā al-banāt*, 3669

In these two verses Allah ﷻ informs us about four scary, terrifying, and frightening events that will take place on that Day.

1.

"On the Day We will set the mountains in motion..." Meaning, imagine that day when We will uproot the mountains from their places and pulverize them into fine particles of dust, as if they had never existed before. This will be an extraordinary sight; something that will strike terror and fear into the hearts of those who will see it. Mountains are the strongest and largest naturally occurring physical structures that we can see. They're symbols of strength and stability and are considered to be immovable and indestructible. But, on that day they will be turned into fine particles of dust. This is a common scene that is described from the Day of Judgment. Allah ﷻ says, "You will see the mountains and think they are firmly fixed, but they will float away like clouds: this is the handiwork of God who has perfected all things."[108] Allah ﷻ also says, "When the earth will be violently shaken, and the mountains are ground to powder, and turn to scattered dust."[109]

2.

"And you will see the earth as an open plain." Meaning, we will see the Earth fully exposed. Nothing will be on it; it will be completely empty. There will be no place for anyone to hide. It will be one big, flat surface without any hills, valleys, trees, mountains, structures, or buildings.

3.

"And We will gather them, and leave none of them behind." Every single human being from the beginning of time till the end of time, big and small, young and old, believers and non-believers will be gathered and held accountable for what they did in this world. Allah ﷻ tells us something very similar in Sūrah al-Wāqiah. "Say, 'Indeed the former and the later peoples are to be gathered together for the appointment of a known Day.'"[110] Allah ﷻ also says in Sūrah Hūd, "That is a Day for which the people will be collected,

---

108 27:88 وَتَرَى الْجِبَالَ تَحْسَبُهَا جَامِدَةً وَهِيَ تَمُرُّ مَرَّ السَّحَابِ ۚ صُنْعَ اللَّهِ الَّذِي أَتْقَنَ كُلَّ شَيْءٍ

109 56:4-6 إِذَا رُجَّتِ الْأَرْضُ رَجًّا * وَبُسَّتِ الْجِبَالُ بَسًّا * فَكَانَتْ هَبَاءً مُنْبَثًّا

110 56:49-50 قُلْ إِنَّ الْأَوَّلِينَ وَالْآخِرِينَ * لَمَجْمُوعُونَ إِلَىٰ مِيقَاتِ يَوْمٍ مَعْلُومٍ

and that is a Day [which will be] witnessed."[111]

4.

"They will be lined up before your Lord in rows. Indeed you have come to Us as We created you the first time. Nay, but you claimed that We would never appoint a time for you." All of mankind will be brought in front of Allah ﷻ at once in rows. The commentators mention that people will be lined up in rows just as they are for prayer. Each row will be occupied by a particular religious community. And then it will be said to them, "Indeed you have come to Us as We created you the first time. Nay, but you claimed that We would never appoint a time for you." Meaning, just as Allah ﷻ created humanity and brought them into existence from nothing, Allah ﷻ will bring them back to life on the Day of Judgment. They will come before Allah ﷻ in the same state that they were created; barefoot, naked, and alone without any belongings. As Allah ﷻ says in Sūrah al-An'ām, "Now you have come to Us alone, just as We created you the first time, and you have left behind that which We had bestowed upon you."[112] Similarly Ā'ishah ﵂ narrated that the Prophet ﷺ said, "People will be assembled on the Day of Resurrection barefoot, naked, and uncircumcised." I said, "O Messenger of Allah! Will the men and the women be together on that Day; looking at one another?" Upon this the Messenger of Allah ﷺ said, "O Ā'ishah, the matter will be too serious for them to look at one another."[113] Muādh ibn Jabal ﵁ narrated that the Prophet ﷺ said, "Truly Allah ﷻ will call out on the Day of Judgment with a loud voice that is not frightening: 'My servants! I am Allah besides whom there is no being deserving of worship: the Most Merciful of the merciful, the Best of Judges, the Swiftest in accounting. My servants! There is no fear upon you today nor will you grieve. Produce your proofs and make your responses easy. Today you will be questioned and held accountable. My Angels! Place my servants in rows upon their toes for accounting."[114]

In order to feel the severity of the day and to create a greater sense of remorse, regret, and sorrow it will then be said to the non-believer, "Nay,

---

111 11:103 ذَٰلِكَ يَوْمٌ مَّجْمُوعٌ لَّهُ النَّاسُ وَذَٰلِكَ يَوْمٌ مَّشْهُودٌ

112 6:94 وَلَقَدْ جِئْتُمُونَا فُرَادَىٰ كَمَا خَلَقْنَاكُمْ أَوَّلَ مَرَّةٍ وَتَرَكْتُم مَّا خَوَّلْنَاكُمْ وَرَاءَ ظُهُورِكُمْ

113 Muslim, *k. al-jannah wa ṣifah naʿimihā wa ahlihā, b. fanā'a al-dunyā wa bayān al-ḥashr yawm al-qiyāmah,* 2859

114 Qurṭubī, *al-Jāmiʿ li Aḥkām al-Quran*, 13:296

but you claimed that We would never appoint a time for you." Meaning, you believed that this would never happen; that you would never be resurrected and never meet Allah ﷻ, and now here you are. The Sūrah then continues to describe the scene on that day.

VERSE 49

وَوُضِعَ الْكِتَابُ فَتَرَى الْمُجْرِمِينَ مُشْفِقِينَ مِمَّا فِيهِ وَيَقُولُونَ
يَا وَيْلَتَنَا مَالِ هَٰذَا الْكِتَابِ لَا يُغَادِرُ صَغِيرَةً وَلَا كَبِيرَةً إِلَّا
أَحْصَاهَا ۚ وَوَجَدُوا مَا عَمِلُوا حَاضِرًا ۗ وَلَا يَظْلِمُ رَبُّكَ أَحَدًا ﴿٤٩﴾

49 And the book will be set down. Then you will see the guilty fearful of what is in it. And they will say, "Woe to us! What a book this is! It does not leave any deed, small or great, except that it has taken it into account." And they will find whatever they did present [before them]. And your Lord wrongs no one.

"And the book will be set down." The "book" in this verse is referring to the book of deeds; the register in which all our deeds, good and bad, big and small, public and private are recorded. This book of deeds serves as a comprehensive witness and record of whatever we say or do in the life of this world. The book will be set down, meaning it will be given to us on the Day of Judgment. This is the book of deeds we'll receive on the Day of Judgment in our right or left hands. The righteous will receive it in their right hands and the wicked will receive it in their left hands.

We ask Allah ﷻ to make us among those who receive it in their right!

When the mujrimūn, the criminals, receive their books, they will be extremely fearful of what is in it. The fear will be seen on their faces through their expressions because they know that their book of deeds is full of sins and disobedience and that there's no way for them to hide it. They will realize that it is a comprehensive and accurate record and they will fear the consequences. They will feel this severe sense of fear, regret, remorse, embarrassment, helplessness, hopelessness, and sorrow. So they will say, "Woe to us!" May we be cursed! May we be destroyed because of our negligence, disobedience, and sins." This is the cry of one who is worried, fearing the worst after they are caught red-handed and unable to evade the consequences of their poor decisions. In their frustration, regret, and remorse they will say, "What a book this is! It does not leave any deed, small or great, except that it has taken it into account." This is an expression of absolute amazement and extreme shock. What a book! It hasn't left out anything, big or small, good or bad, significant or insignificant, except that it has been recorded in it. They fear both punishment from Allah ﷻ and disgrace in the eyes of other people. "And they will find whatever they did present [before them]."

Allah ﷻ tells us this elsewhere in the Quran as well. Allah ﷻ tells us in Sūrah Āl Imrān, "The Day every soul will find what it has done of good present [before it] and what it has done of evil, it will wish that between itself and that [evil] was a great distance. And Allah warns you of Himself, and Allah is Kind to [His] servants."[115] Allah ﷻ also says, "Man will be informed that Day of what he sent ahead and kept back."[116]

Accountability, judgment, reward and punishment are all built upon the infinite and absolute justice of Allah ﷻ. "And your Lord wrongs no one." Absolute justice and equality will be established on the Day of Resurrection. No individual will be wronged whatsoever and everyone will receive their rights in full. He ﷻ will judge between His creatures for all of their deeds, and He will not treat any of His creatures with injustice. He ﷻ will overlook, pardon, forgive, and have mercy upon whomever He wills as an expression of His infinite mercy. He ﷻ will hold accountable and punish whomever He wills

115 3:30 يَوْمَ تَجِدُ كُلُّ نَفْسٍ مَّا عَمِلَتْ مِنْ خَيْرٍ مُّحْضَرًا وَمَا عَمِلَتْ مِن سُوءٍ تَوَدُّ لَوْ أَنَّ بَيْنَهَا وَبَيْنَهُ أَمَدًا بَعِيدًا ۗ وَيُحَذِّرُكُمُ اللَّهُ نَفْسَهُ ۗ وَاللَّهُ رَءُوفٌ بِالْعِبَادِ

116 75:13 يُنَبَّأُ الْإِنسَانُ يَوْمَئِذٍ بِمَا قَدَّمَ وَأَخَّرَ

by His power, wisdom, and justice. He ﷻ will fill Hell with the disbelievers and those who have been disobedient. Then, He will rescue the disobedient believers, and leave the disbelievers there for eternity. He ﷻ is the Judge Who never wrongs or oppresses. Allah ﷻ says, "He does not wrong anyone by as much as the weight of a speck of dust: He doubles any good deed and gives a tremendous reward of His own."[117] Allah ﷻ also says, "We will set up scales of justice for the Day of Resurrection so that no one can be wronged in the least, and if there should be even the weight of a mustard seed, We shall bring it out- We take excellent account."[118]

As a quick reminder, the last set of verses gave us a very powerful and profound example of the reality of the life of this world. We're reminded in a very brief, yet powerful way, that the life of this world is temporary and fleeting; that it will very quickly come to an end. And that the life to come, the life of the Hereafter, is a life of eternity. The Quran wants to change our perspective; it wants to change the way we view the material world. It wants us to recognize that the material is impermanent; whereas, belief and righteous deeds are permanent. We're reminded that, just like anything else in this world, we too will one day cease to exist. So we shouldn't be fooled, deceived, and tricked by the life of this world. Rather, we should focus on what is everlasting; those things that will benefit us in this world and more importantly in the next. The passage ended with a brief description of some events that will take place on the Day of Judgment.

Now the Sūrah transitions into the story of Adam ﷺ and Satan's refusal to prostrate to him. This particular story is mentioned in the Quran a number of times. For example, it's mentioned in Sūrah al-Baqarah, Sūrah al-Arāf, Sūrah al-Ḥijr, and Sūrah Ṣād. However, each time it is mentioned for a different reason. The story is mentioned very briefly here as an admonition to the wealthy and proud Makkans, reminding them that Satan's refusal to prostrate before Adam ﷺ was based similarly on pride and a false sense of superiority. Allah ﷻ is highlighting the parallels between their attitudes towards Islam and the Muslims and the attitude of Satan.

---

117 4:40 إِنَّ اللَّهَ لَا يَظْلِمُ مِثْقَالَ ذَرَّةٍ ۖ وَإِن تَكُ حَسَنَةً يُضَاعِفْهَا وَيُؤْتِ مِن لَّدُنْهُ أَجْرًا عَظِيمًا

118 21:47 وَنَضَعُ الْمَوَازِينَ الْقِسْطَ لِيَوْمِ الْقِيَامَةِ فَلَا تُظْلَمُ نَفْسٌ شَيْئًا ۖ وَإِن كَانَ مِثْقَالَ حَبَّةٍ مِّنْ خَرْدَلٍ أَتَيْنَا بِهَا ۗ وَكَفَىٰ بِنَا حَاسِبِينَ

VERSE 50

وَإِذْ قُلْنَا لِلْمَلَائِكَةِ اسْجُدُوا لِآدَمَ فَسَجَدُوا إِلَّا إِبْلِيسَ كَانَ مِنَ
الْجِنِّ فَفَسَقَ عَنْ أَمْرِ رَبِّهِ ۗ أَفَتَتَّخِذُونَهُ وَذُرِّيَّتَهُ أَوْلِيَاءَ مِنْ دُونِي
وَهُمْ لَكُمْ عَدُوٌّ ۚ بِئْسَ لِلظَّالِمِينَ بَدَلًا ﴿٥٠﴾

50 (Remember) when We said to the angels, "Bow before Adam." So, they all bowed down except for Iblīs (Satan) who was one of the Jinn. So he rebelled against the command of his Lord. Will you then take him and his progeny as protectors apart from Me, though they are an enemy to you? How evil an exchange for the wrongdoers!

Allah ﷻ is reminding us about the enmity of Satan; just as he was an enemy to Adam عليه السلام he is also our sworn and mortal enemy. This verse is describing a scene from the world of the unseen after the creation of Adam عليه السلام. Allah ﷻ is telling His Messenger ﷺ to remind people of when He ordered all of the Angels to bow down to Adam عليه السلام out of respect and honor. All of the Angels immediately bowed down except for Iblīs, who was among the Jinn. He refused to bow before Adam عليه السلام because he was fooled by his own arrogance and pride.

Before his fall from grace, Iblīs was a devoted servant of Allah ﷻ. He was so special that he was granted permission to attend the gatherings of the angels. The main reasons why he didn't bow down were arrogance, pride, and jealousy. He thought he was better than Adam عليه السلام because he was created from fire whereas Adam was created from clay. As Allah tells us in Sūrah al-Arāf, "Allah asked, 'What prevented you from bowing down when I commanded you?' He replied, 'I am better than he is: You created me from fire and him from clay.'"[119] His pride, arrogance, and jealousy caused him to disobey Allah ﷻ. Pride is one of the most dangerous diseases of the heart.

The word for pride in Arabic is kibr. Linguistically the word kibr is derived from the root letters ك ب ر , which convey the meaning of growth, either in mass or age. When a person is arrogant or prideful they glorify themselves and think of themselves as someone great or important. As a spiritual disease, scholars throughout history have tried to capture its reality through a number of definitions.

First and foremost, the Prophet ﷺ defined الكبر as, "denial of the truth and dislike for others."[120] al-Zubaydī رحمه الله defined it as, "A state or condition where a person thinks good of themselves (admires themselves) and they consider themselves to be better than others."[121] Imām al-Ghazālī رحمه الله defines it as self-aggrandizement and thinking you're better than others.[122] al-Jāhiẓ رحمه الله said, "When a person thinks highly of themselves (self-aggrandizement), considers their qualities to be good, belittles others, and behaves arrogantly with one whom they should be humble with."[123] Imām al-Ghazālī رحمه الله also says, "The reality of arrogance is that you see yourself as being superior to others in possessing attributes of perfection. So there occurs in you haughtiness and a delightful sensation from this view and belief..."

Kibr is to think that we're better than others because of our knowledge, wealth, lineage, race, color, power, strength, or language. In *Iḥyā'a ʿUlūm al-Dīn*, Imām al-Ghazālī رحمه الله writes very beautifully, "Arrogance/Pride is an extremely grave calamity. Through it, distinguished people are destroyed. Rarely are worshippers, ascetics and scholars free from it, let alone normal people. How can it not be a grave calamity when the Prophet ﷺ said, "No one who has an atom's weight of arrogance in his heart will enter Paradise." It's a barrier in front of Paradise because it separates between a person and all the characteristics of true believers. Those characteristics are the gates to paradise and arrogance closes all of those gates. Because a person who has

---

119 7:12 قَالَ مَا مَنَعَكَ أَلَّا تَسْجُدَ إِذْ أَمَرْتُكَ ۖ قَالَ أَنَا خَيْرٌ مِّنْهُ خَلَقْتَنِي مِن نَّارٍ وَخَلَقْتَهُ مِن طِينٍ

120 Muslim, *k. al-īmān, b. taḥrīm al-kibr wa bayānihi*, 91

121 حالة يتخصص بها الإنسان من إعجابه بنفسه، وأن يرى نفسه أكبر من غيره

122 استعظام النفس، ورؤية قدرها فوق قدر الغير

123 استعظام الإنسان نفسه، و استحسان ما فيه من الفضائل، والإستهانة بالناس، واستصغارهم، والترفع على من يجب التواضع له

arrogance is unable to love for the believer what they love for themself. An arrogant person is compelled to have all the blameworthy traits to protect his pride. There isn't a praiseworthy characteristic except that they're unable to adopt it out of fear of losing their honor..."[124]

He also writes, "Arrogance bars you from the entirety of praiseworthy manners, because the proud person is not capable of loving for people what he loves for himself. Nor is he capable of modesty, or leaving disdain, envy or anger. Likewise he's incapable of concealing rage, giving good counsel or leaving ostentation. On the whole, there does not remain any bad trait except that the arrogant person is compelled to perpetrate it, and there does not remain any good trait except that he is compelled to leave it."[125]

The most villainous and evil individuals throughout history were filled with arrogance and false pride: Satan, Pharaoh, the enemies of the Prophet ﷺ, and every single tyrant throughout history. Perhaps that's why there are so many verses of the Quran and narrations from the Prophet ﷺ that condemn pride and arrogance. For example the Prophet ﷺ said, "He who has in his heart the weight of a mustard seed of pride shall not enter Paradise." A person said, "Verily a person loves that his dress should be fine, and his shoes should be fine." He ﷺ responded, "Verily, Allah is Graceful and He loves Grace. Pride is to disdain the truth (out of self-conceit) and have contempt for the people."[126] The Prophet ﷺ also said, "Whoever has humility Allah will elevate him, and whoever is arrogant Allah will lower him."[127] May Allah ﷻ protect us from pride and arrogance and make us amongst the people of humility.

Satan's pride and arrogance led him to disobey the direct command of Allah ﷻ. "So he rebelled against the command of his Lord." The verb used for rebelling here is فَسَقَ, which literally means to stray from the right course or to behave sinfully. In the context of Islam, it refers to open disobedience; leaving the obedience of Allah ﷻ. That's exactly what Iblīs did; he openly disobeyed the command of Allah ﷻ.

Allah ﷻ then reprimands and scolds those people who choose to follow Satan by consciously choosing to disbelieve, reject the truth, oppose prophets

124 Al-Ghazālī, *Iḥyā' ʿUlūm al-Dīn*, 3:344

125 Ibid

126 Muslim, *k. al-īmān, b. taḥrīm al-kibr wa bayānihi*, 91

127 Haythamī, *Majmaʿ al-Zawā'id*, 10:328

and messengers, follow their desires, sin, and engage in acts of disobedience even though Satan is their sworn, open enemy. He ﷻ reprimands them by asking them a rhetorical question. Oftentimes rhetorical questions are used to scold and reprimand individuals in order to make them realize their mistakes. Allah ﷻ says, "Will you then take him and his progeny as protectors apart from Me, though they are an enemy to you? How evil an exchange for the wrongdoers!" This is also an expression of wonder and amazement; how in the world can you take Satan and his progeny as protectors apart from Me? Meaning, how can you obey and follow Satan, while he's an open and sworn enemy of humanity? His sole purpose and objective in life is to misguide as many people as possible and lead as many people as he can to eternal damnation. That's the oath he took in front of Allah ﷻ as mentioned in Sūrah al-Arāf when Satan said, "Because You have put me in the wrong, I will lie in wait for them all on Your straight path. I will come at them- from their front and their back, from their right and their left- and You will find that most of them are ungrateful."[128]

After refusing to bow before Adam ﵇, Iblīs asked Allah ﷻ to give him some time; a little bit of a reprieve. Allah ﷻ tells us in Sūrah al-Arāf that Satan said, "Grant me respite until the Day they are resurrected." He ﷻ said, "Truly you are among those granted respite."[129]

Satan is not our friend. Allah ﷻ makes this explicitly clear throughout the Quran. Allah ﷻ tells us, "Truly Satan is your enemy so treat him as an enemy."[130] The Prophet ﷺ said, "Iblīs places his throne upon water; he then sends detachments (for creating dissension); the nearer to him in rank are those who are most notorious in creating dissension. One of them comes and says: 'I did such and such.' And he says, 'You have done nothing.' Then one amongst them comes and says, 'I did not spare so and so until I sowed the seed of discord between a husband and a wife.' Satan goes near him and says, 'You have done well.'"[131] Allah ﷻ ends the verse in Sūrah al-Kahf by highlighting how ridiculous it is for someone to follow Satan and his helpers. "How

---

128 7:16-17 قَالَ فَبِمَا أَغْوَيْتَنِي لَأَقْعُدَنَّ لَهُمْ صِرَاطَكَ الْمُسْتَقِيمَ * ثُمَّ لَآتِيَنَّهُم مِّن بَيْنِ أَيْدِيهِمْ وَمِنْ خَلْفِهِمْ وَعَنْ أَيْمَانِهِمْ وَعَن شَمَائِلِهِمْ ۖ وَلَا تَجِدُ أَكْثَرَهُمْ شَاكِرِينَ

129 7:14-15 قَالَ أَنظِرْنِي إِلَىٰ يَوْمِ يُبْعَثُونَ * قَالَ إِنَّكَ مِنَ الْمُنظَرِينَ

130 35:36 إِنَّ الشَّيْطَانَ لَكُمْ عَدُوٌّ فَاتَّخِذُوهُ عَدُوًّا

131 Muslim, *k. ṣifah al-qiyāmah wa al-jannah wa al-nār, b. taḥrīsh al-shayṭān wa baʿthihi sarāyāhu lī fitnah al-nās wa anna maʿa kull insān qarīn*, 2813

evil an exchange for the wrongdoers!" The exchange is referring to taking Satan and his helpers as protectors and guardians beside Allah ﷻ. Meaning, instead of obeying Allah ﷻ they disobey Him by following the path of Satan.

Allah ﷻ then explicitly states that Satan and all these false deities that people have associated with Him have no power or authority whatsoever. They're completely helpless themselves.

مَّا أَشْهَدتُّهُمْ خَلْقَ السَّمَاوَاتِ وَالْأَرْضِ وَلَا خَلْقَ أَنفُسِهِمْ وَمَا
كُنتُ مُتَّخِذَ الْمُضِلِّينَ عَضُدًا ﴿٥١﴾

[51] I did not make them witnesses to the creation of the heavens and the earth, nor to their own creation. And I do not take as My supporters those who lead others astray.

According to some commentators, Allah ﷻ is referring to those beings or objects that people associate as partners with Allah ﷻ. Allah ﷻ is making it absolutely clear that these false deities - Satan and his ilk - didn't witness the creation of the heavens and the earth. Meaning they weren't partners with Allah ﷻ in creation, rather they are creations of Allah ﷻ themselves, so it's illogical for them to be partners with Allah ﷻ in being worshipped. Similarly, Allah ﷻ didn't make them witness their own creation; meaning they are creatures themselves that don't deserve to be worshipped.

While explaining this verse, Ibn Kathīr ﵀ writes, "Allah says, 'These whom you take as helpers instead of Me are creatures just like you. They do not possess anything and did not witness the creation of heaven and earth, because they did not exist at that time.' Allah says, 'I am the One Who independently and exclusively creates and controls all things, and I have no partner, associate, or advisor in that.'"[132] Essentially this verse is highlighting the concept of tawḥīd while at the same time highlighting the absurdity of associating partners with Allah ﷻ.

Allah ﷻ ends the verse by declaring that He wouldn't take them as helpers. "I do not take as My supporters those who lead others astray." Allah ﷻ did not seek their help, nor would He seek their help, because He alone is the Almighty and All-Powerful, the One who is not in need of anything and everything is in need of Him ﷻ. Syed Quṭb ﵀ comments, "Sublime and great is God. He is in no need of anyone in the universe. He is the Almighty who has the power to accomplish whatever He wills. The phraseology here is intentional. It brings to the fore the myths of the unbelievers only to shoot them down. Those who seek protection from Satan and make him a partner to God only do so because they imagine that Satan has a great wealth of knowledge and overpowering might, when in fact Satan is a seducer who leads people astray. God does not like deviation or those who lead other people astray. Had He, for argument's sake, sought helpers, He would not have taken them from among the seducers who lead people into error and deviation. This is the meaning of the verse and its ending aim to emphasize."[133]

The Sūrah then paints another scene from the Day of Judgment, highlighting the consequence that awaits those who associate partners with Allah ﷻ.

132 ibn Kathīr, *Tafsīr al-Quran al-ʿAẓīm*, 9:155

133 Quṭb, *fī Ẓilāl al-Quran*, 4:2275

VERSE 52

وَيَوْمَ يَقُولُ نَادُوا شُرَكَاءِيَ الَّذِينَ زَعَمْتُمْ فَدَعَوْهُمْ فَلَمْ يَسْتَجِيبُوا
لَهُمْ وَجَعَلْنَا بَيْنَهُم مَّوْبِقًا ﴿٥٢﴾

52 On the Day when He says, "Call those who you claimed as My partners," they will call upon them, but they will not respond to them, and We will place a gulf between them.

In this verse, Allah ﷻ is telling Muhammad ﷺ to tell the non-believers that on the Day of Judgment Allah ﷻ will scold, reprimand, and disgrace them as a consequence of their poor choices. Allah ﷻ will tell them to call their false deities whom they associated with Allah ﷻ and claimed were His partners so that they can save them from the difficulties of that day and eternal punishment. "Call those who you claimed as My partners." They will call out to their false deities, but they will not respond. There will be a deafening silence.

This is one of several verses in the Quran that highlight that on the Day of Judgment Allah ﷻ will challenge those who associate partners with Him to call upon them for help and intercession. On that day, those partners will abandon them, dissociate from them, and will be unable to help them in any way. This will be said to them as a reprimand and rebuke in order to scold them and make them feel a greater sense of regret and remorse. "And We will place a gulf between them." The "gulf" between them may refer to a place of destruction or a valley of Hell into which those who associate partners to Allah ﷻ will be cast. Allah ﷻ then tells us of the consequences of their disbelief and shirk.

VERSE 53

وَرَأَى الْمُجْرِمُونَ النَّارَ فَظَنُّوا أَنَّهُم مُّوَاقِعُوهَا وَلَمْ يَجِدُوا عَنْهَا مَصْرِفًا ﴿٥٣﴾

[53] The Guilty will see the Fire, and know they will fall into it, but they will find no means of escape from it.

Al-Mujrimūn, the guilty or the criminals, those that are guilty of disbelief, sin, disobedience, and immorality will see the Fire of Hell with their own two eyes. Once they see it they will have absolute certainty that they "will fall into it." There will be no way for them to escape from their destiny. They will have no place to run and hide, seek safety, refuge, and protection. They will have no one to help them and protect them from the Fire.

In this next set of verses, Allah ﷻ covers a number of different topics starting with describing one aspect of the Quran.

VERSE 54

وَلَقَدْ صَرَّفْنَا فِي هَٰذَا الْقُرْآنِ لِلنَّاسِ مِن كُلِّ مَثَلٍ ۚ وَكَانَ الْإِنسَانُ أَكْثَرَ شَيْءٍ جَدَلًا ﴿٥٤﴾

54 And indeed We have employed every kind of parable for mankind in this Quran. And man is the most contentious of beings.

This is a very beautiful verse in which Allah ﷻ gives us a holistic macro understanding of the Quran. "And indeed We have employed every kind of parable for mankind in this Quran." A parable is an example, or a metaphor, that is used by Allah ﷻ in the Quran to provide us with lessons and guidance. They are known as amthāl al-Quran. A parable is defined as a short allegorical story designed to illustrate or teach some truth, religious principle, or moral lesson. The word used for parable in Arabic is mathal, which is translated as an example, metaphor or allegory. Allah ﷻ says in Sūrah al-Zumar, "And We have certainly presented for the people in this Qur'an from every [kind of] example - that they might remember."[134]

These examples provide us with reminders, lessons, encouragement, reprimand, reflection, contemplation, ease understanding, and illustrate difficult concepts with something tangible. Allah ﷻ uses amthāl to help us understand concepts such as faith, patience, gratitude, morality, ethics, values, reliance, life, death, and resurrection.

In this verse, Allah ﷻ is telling us that He has clearly explained and clarified every single thing that we as human beings need to know, to live well in this life and the next, so that we can know and recognize the path of truth

134 39:27  وَلَقَدْ ضَرَبْنَا لِلنَّاسِ فِي هَٰذَا الْقُرْآنِ مِن كُلِّ مَثَلٍ لَّعَلَّهُمْ يَتَذَكَّرُونَ

and guidance. The Quran contains guidance for every single thing we need to know as human beings in order to achieve success in this life and more importantly in the life to come. Allah ﷻ describes the Quran in Sūrah Yūsuf as "an elaboration of all things." The full verse is, "Certainly in their stories is a lesson for those possessed of intellect. It is not a fabricated account; rather, it is a confirmation of that which came before it, and an elaboration of all things, and a guidance and mercy for a people who believe."[135]

The Quran is our book of guidance; it's our roadmap to happiness in this world and salvation in the Hereafter. That's why it's so important for us to have a real, daily, practical, and intimate relationship with the Quran. We have to read it, contemplate over its meanings, and internalize its message. That's why the Quran was revealed - to reflect, ponder and contemplate over its meanings. Alī رضي الله عنه said, "Indeed there's no good in worship without fiqh, there's no good in knowledge without understanding, and there's no good in recitation without contemplation."[136] The more we engage with the book of Allah ﷻ, the more we learn and the more we understand.

It's such a book that its wonders are never ending, it never becomes boring through repetition. Whoever speaks from it will speak the truth, whoever rules with it will be just, and whoever holds fast to it will be guided to the straight path. That's why ibn Abbās رضي الله عنه said, "If I lost the rope of my camel I would find it in the book of Allah!"[137]

Despite the fact that the Quran is a book of guidance and that it contains everything we need as human beings, Allah ﷻ tells us some of the reasons why some people still fail to take advantage of it or benefit from it. "And man is the most contentious of beings." Meaning, despite the clarity of the Quran, its guidance, its light, and its details human beings still choose to oppose and argue against the truth. Part of the nature of disbelief is to reject the truth and argue against it with stubbornness and pride. Even though Allah ﷻ has explained everything necessary in detail, mankind is still predisposed to argument and dispute. That is why we find a lot of people who choose to reject the truth and disbelieve. This argumentative nature will be on display on the Day of Judgment as well. Anas رضي الله عنه narrates that once while they were

---

135 12:111 لَقَدْ كَانَ فِي قَصَصِهِمْ عِبْرَةٌ لِّأُولِي الْأَلْبَابِ ۗ مَا كَانَ حَدِيثًا يُفْتَرَىٰ وَلَٰكِن تَصْدِيقَ الَّذِي بَيْنَ يَدَيْهِ وَتَفْصِيلَ كُلِّ شَيْءٍ وَهُدًى وَرَحْمَةً لِّقَوْمٍ يُؤْمِنُونَ

136 al-Qaraḍāwī, *Kayf Nataʿāmal mʿā al-Quran al-ʿAẓīm*, 169

137 al-Ālusī, *Rūḥ al-Maʿānī*, 14:98

in the company of the Prophet ﷺ he smiled and asked, "Do you know why I smiled?" The companions responded, "Allah and His Messenger know best." He ﷺ said, "I remembered a conversation that a servant will have with his Lord. He (the servant) will say, 'My Lord, have you not guaranteed me protection against injustice?' He ﷻ will say, 'Of course.' Then the servant will say, 'I will not allow any witness against me but myself.' He ﷻ will say, 'Your self is a sufficient witness against you and the two Recording Angels are sufficient witnesses against you.' Then a seal will be placed over his mouth and it will be said to his hands and feet to speak and they will speak of his deeds. Then the mouth will be free to speak, and he would say (to the hands and feet), 'Away with you! May Allah curse you! I had argued only on your behalf.'"[138]

Allah ﷻ then tells us that oftentimes people refuse to believe because of two reasons:

1. They are waiting for punishment, or
2. They want to see the punishment of the Hereafter with their own eyes.

138 Muslim, *k. al-zuhd wa al-raqā'iq*, 2969

VERSE 55

وَمَا مَنَعَ النَّاسَ أَن يُؤْمِنُوا إِذْ جَاءَهُمُ الْهُدَىٰ وَيَسْتَغْفِرُوا رَبَّهُمْ
إِلَّا أَن تَأْتِيَهُمْ سُنَّةُ الْأَوَّلِينَ أَوْ يَأْتِيَهُمُ الْعَذَابُ قُبُلًا ﴿٥٥﴾

55 And nothing prevents men from believing when guidance comes to them and from seeking forgiveness from their Lord, except that [they wait] for what befell earlier generations to come to them, or the punishment to come upon them face to face.

This verse is referring specifically to the non-believers of Makkah but is applicable to anyone who rejects and denies the truth after it has been clarified to them. Allah ﷻ is telling us that nothing prevented the non-believers of Makkah from accepting faith after having witnessed clear signs and proofs regarding the existence and oneness of Allah ﷻ and the messengership of Muhammad ﷺ, and seeking forgiveness from their Lord except for two things:

1.

Being afflicted with punishment and destruction like the previous nations, or

2.

Seeing and experiencing the punishment of the Hereafter with their own eyes. Meaning, they're waiting to see if the same worldly punishment that befell earlier people will come upon them as well or to witness the punishment of the Hereafter with their own two eyes. What this means is that they won't believe or accept faith until they are punished. Everything has already been explained to them; there's no reason for them to reject or deny the truth. They have received guidance in plenty, which should have been sufficient for them to believe and follow Allah's orders. But they demanded for themselves the sort of suffering that befell nations of old. They made such a demand thinking that Allah's punishment would never overtake them, or they did so in mockery. For example, they said, "O Allah! If this is indeed the truth from You, then rain down stones upon us from the sky or overcome us with a painful punishment."[139] Sometimes they modified their demands, asking for the punishment to be shown directly to them. They argued - with pride, arrogance, ignorance, and stubbornness - that this would prove what the Prophets preached and then they would believe in them. However, punishment comes from Allah ﷻ, not the Messenger, and that's why Allah ﷻ says next,

وَمَا نُرْسِلُ الْمُرْسَلِينَ إِلَّا مُبَشِّرِينَ وَمُنذِرِينَ ۚ وَيُجَادِلُ الَّذِينَ
كَفَرُوا بِالْبَاطِلِ لِيُدْحِضُوا بِهِ الْحَقَّ ۖ وَاتَّخَذُوا آيَاتِي وَمَا أُنذِرُوا
هُزُوًا ﴿٥٦﴾

[56] And We don't send the Messenger except as bearers of glad tidings and as warners. And those who disbelieve dis-

139 8:32 وَإِذْ قَالُوا اللَّهُمَّ إِن كَانَ هَٰذَا هُوَ الْحَقَّ مِنْ عِندِكَ فَأَمْطِرْ عَلَيْنَا حِجَارَةً مِّنَ السَّمَاءِ أَوِ ائْتِنَا بِعَذَابٍ أَلِيمٍ

pute falsely in order to refute the truth. They take My signs and that which they have been warned as mockery.

The word mursalīn is translated as messengers and refers to all of the previous prophets and messengers that were sent by Allah ﷻ throughout history. This verse is telling us that their role or function was to convey the message of Allah ﷻ that was revealed to them. That included giving glad tidings of forgiveness, reward, and paradise for those who believed and warnings of punishment and sin for those who rejected the truth. However, despite receiving the message and recognizing its truth they decided to argue against it. "And those who disbelieve dispute falsely in order to refute the truth." The disbelievers respond to the message with rejection and opposition. They argue against it not because they're right; rather, because they want to refute the truth. And since they're unable to refute the truth they resort to mockery and derision. "They take My signs and that which they have been warned as mockery." They treat the Quran, revelation, miracles, evidence, and proof of Allah's existence and oneness as a joke; something to be taken lightly and made fun of. This is the worst kind of rejection and denial. It's an attitude of arrogance and ignorance. Imagine hearing the truth, recognizing it, and then rejecting it through mockery and ridicule because of pride, arrogance, and stubbornness.

After explaining the reason for their disbelief and their mockery, Allah ﷻ describes the non-believers with some characteristics that bring them disgrace and dishonor.

وَمَنْ أَظْلَمُ مِمَّن ذُكِّرَ بِآيَاتِ رَبِّهِ فَأَعْرَضَ عَنْهَا وَنَسِيَ مَا
قَدَّمَتْ يَدَاهُ ۚ إِنَّا جَعَلْنَا عَلَىٰ قُلُوبِهِمْ أَكِنَّةً أَن يَفْقَهُوهُ وَفِي آذَانِهِمْ

وَقْـرًا ۖ وَإِن تَدْعُهُـمْ إِلَى الْهُـدَىٰ فَلَـن يَهْتَـدُوا إِذًا أَبَـدًا ﴿٥٧﴾

[57] And who does greater wrong than one who has been reminded of the signs of his Lord, then turns away from them and forgets that which his hands have sent forth? Surely We have placed coverings over their hearts, such that they understand it not, and in their ears a deafness. Even if you call them to guidance, they will never be rightly guided.

There is no injustice greater than disbelief, especially after witnessing the signs and evidence of the truth and then turning away from them. They are heedless and careless of what they do in this world. Oftentimes, we forget how great of a sin and injustice disbelief truly is; we don't recognize the gravity of rejecting and refusing to accept the truth. There's no sin greater than disbelief. The rhetorical question mentioned at the beginning of the verse, "and who does greater wrong than the one who has been reminded of the signs of his Lord, then turns away from them and forgets that which his hands have sent forth", is repeated throughout the Quran. It's usually asked in relation to those who deny the signs of Allah ﷻ. Allah ﷻ is telling us that there's absolutely no one worse or more disgraceful than a person who turns away from His signs that invite them towards the truth, success, and salvation.

Additionally, they forget about the consequences of their actions or they don't care about the consequences. "And forgets that which his hands have sent forth." They say what they want and do what they want without any thought or apprehension. This is the absolute most unjust type of person; they're not just to themselves nor are they just in their relationship with Allah ﷻ. As a consequence of their disbelief, rejection, stubbornness, and disobedience, Allah ﷻ places a seal over their hearts and ears. "Surely We have placed coverings over their hearts, such that they understand it not, and in their ears a deafness. Even if you call them to guidance, they will never be rightly guided." Their hearts are covered and veiled from recognizing and understanding the truth, as a result of their own conscious decisions.

The heart within the Islamic tradition has been given a lot of importance. It's considered to be the center of understanding and enlightenment. It's the center of faith, belief, reliance, and comprehension; true recognition of the truth. Modern science attributes this to the mind and the intellect but we understand it to be the spiritual heart. The heart is "a subtle tenuous substance of an ethereal spiritual sort, which is connected with the physical heart. This subtle tenuous substance is the real essence of man. The heart is the part of man that perceives and knows and experiences; it is addressed, punished, rebuked, and held responsible..." The heart in the Islamic tradition is the center of being, intellect and consciousness.

Those who turn away from Allah ﷻ, reject the truth and engage in sin and disobedience, a seal is placed over their hearts. They're no longer able to perceive and recognize the truth; they can't tell right from wrong. Similarly a "deafness" is placed in their ears. Meaning they hear the truth being spoken, but they're unable to understand, process, and comprehend it. That's why Allah ﷻ then consoles and comforts the Prophet ﷺ by telling him that if he invites them towards guidance, they will never be guided. Again this is a result and consequence of their own actions and choices. Allah ﷻ tells us this elsewhere in the Quran as well. For example, in Sūrah al-Muṭaffifīn Allah ﷻ says, "But no! In fact, their hearts have been stained by all [the evil] they used to commit!"[140] Allah ﷻ also says, "Allah has sealed their hearts and their hearing, and their sight is covered. They will suffer a tremendous punishment."[141] Syed Quṭb رحمه الله writes, "These people who treat what Allah has bestowed from on high with mockery and who ridicule His warnings cannot understand the Quran or comprehend its message. Hence, Allah places over their hearts screens which prevent them from understanding it. In their ears He causes a sort of deafness so that they cannot hear it. He has also willed that, because of their deliberate refusal and willful turning away from His guidance, they will never be guided. For guidance to penetrate people's hearts, such hearts must be open to receive it in the first place."[142]

Despite their pride, arrogance, ignorance, stubbornness and refusal to accept the truth, Allah ﷻ in His infinite mercy delays their punishment. He gives them time to reflect, ponder, think, recognize their mistakes and

---

140 83:14 كَلَّا ۖ بَلْ ۜ رَانَ عَلَىٰ قُلُوبِهِم مَّا كَانُوا يَكْسِبُونَ

141 2:7 خَتَمَ اللَّهُ عَلَىٰ قُلُوبِهِمْ وَعَلَىٰ سَمْعِهِمْ ۖ وَعَلَىٰ أَبْصَارِهِمْ غِشَاوَةٌ ۖ وَلَهُمْ عَذَابٌ عَظِيمٌ

142 Quṭb, *fī Ẓilāl al-Quran*, 4:2276

repent.

VERSE 58

وَرَبُّكَ الْغَفُورُ ذُو الرَّحْمَةِ ۖ لَوْ يُؤَاخِذُهُم بِمَا كَسَبُوا لَعَجَّلَ لَهُمُ
الْعَذَابَ ۚ بَل لَّهُم مَّوْعِدٌ لَّن يَجِدُوا مِن دُونِهِ مَوْئِلًا ﴿٥٨﴾

58 And your Lord is All-Forgiving, full of mercy. Were he to take them to task for that which they have earned, He would have hastened the punishment for them. Nay, but theirs is an appointed time, beyond which they shall find no refuge.

Allah ﷻ is al-Ghafūr, the All-Forgiving, and al-Raḥīm, the Possessor of infinite and limitless mercy. He ﷻ forgives regardless of how much a person has sinned or how major or grave the sin is. And He ﷻ continues to forgive as long as a person turns back to Him in forgiveness and repentance. His ﷻ mercy is infinite; it encompasses every single thing in this universe. If Allah ﷻ wanted to, He could have held people accountable for what they've done immediately. If that were the case, He would have brought punishment upon them in this world without any delay. As Allah ﷻ tells us in Sūrah Fātir, "If Allah were to punish people [immediately] for what they have committed, He would not have left a single living being on earth. But He delays them for an appointed term. And when their time arrives, then surely Allah is All-Seeing of His servants."[143] Instead, Allah ﷻ has set an appointed time for their punishment, which can come in this world or the

143 35:45 وَلَوْ يُؤَاخِذُ اللَّهُ النَّاسَ بِمَا كَسَبُوا مَا تَرَكَ عَلَىٰ ظَهْرِهَا مِن دَابَّةٍ وَلَٰكِن يُؤَخِّرُهُمْ إِلَىٰ أَجَلٍ مُّسَمًّى ۖ فَإِذَا جَاءَ أَجَلُهُمْ فَإِنَّ اللَّهَ كَانَ بِعِبَادِهِ بَصِيرًا

next. It's up to Allah ﷻ.

VERSE 59

وَتِلْكَ الْقُرَىٰ أَهْلَكْنَاهُمْ لَمَّا ظَلَمُوا وَجَعَلْنَا لِمَهْلِكِهِم مَّوْعِدًا ﴿٥٩﴾

[59] And those towns, We destroyed them for the wrong they did, and We set an appointed time for their destruction.

Allah ﷻ is reminding the polytheists of Makkah of the past nations and communities that were destroyed because of their rejection and disobedience such as, Ād, Thamūd, and the people of Lūṭ ﷺ. The Quran repeatedly refers to the destruction of whole towns as a result of their disbelief and wrongdoing. All of these references are found in Makkan revelation because they're mostly intended as warnings for the Quraysh of Makkah. This is understood as a veiled threat; you have an appointed time that is set for your punishment, just as these previous nations did.

In the next set of verses, Allah ﷻ relates a very unique and interesting story about Mūsa ﷺ and his encounter and journey with a man of God known as al-Khaḍir[144]. Interestingly this story is not told or hinted at anywhere else in the Quran. Similarly, this is the only account of Mūsa ﷺ in the Quran that doesn't also have some reference in the Biblical tradition. This is the third story mentioned in the Sūrah after the story of the people of the cave and the owner of the two gardens.

In the Sūrah, Allah ﷻ relates only a few events from this story and doesn't provide all the fine details. For example, Allah ﷻ doesn't mention exactly where or when this story took place. We don't know if it took place when Mūsa ﷺ was still in Egypt, or after he escaped from Firawn and his army, or even later on.[145] The Quranic narrative also doesn't mention the name of the individual who Mūsa ﷺ set out to meet. It doesn't mention who he was, where he was from, and whether he was a prophet, scholar, or an ascetic. Allah ﷻ simply describes him as "a servant from among Our servants."

One of the reasons why all of these details are left out is because, in the grand scheme of things, they're not that important. They actually take away

---

144 al-Qurṭubī ؒ is of the opinion that al-Khaḍir was a prophet and brings a few arguments to support his position. The majority of mufassirūn (scholars of Quran interpretation) are of the opinion that al-Khaḍir was not a prophet, but was a very special and pious man of God.

145 Although there is a narration that mentions it took place after Mūsa ﷺ and the Children of Israel returned to Egypt and settled there. See Qurṭubī's *al-Jāmiʿ fī Aḥkā al-Quran*, 13:317.

from the main purpose, objective, and lessons of the story. We're supposed to focus on what lessons, morals, and guidance we can derive from these incidents and not worry about the minute details. However, a more detailed version of this story is found in a ḥadīth recorded in both Ṣaḥīḥ al-Bukhārī and Muslim narrated by Ubayy ibn Kab ﷺ.

Ubayy ibn Kab ﷺ narrates that the Prophet ﷺ said, "Once Mūsa ﷺ was delivering a sermon to the Children of Israel when he was asked, 'Who is the most knowledgeable person?' Mūsa ﷺ wasn't aware of anyone who was more knowledgeable than him so he said, 'I am.' Even though he was right, Allah ﷻ was not pleased with his answer. The situation required that he say Allah ﷻ knows best. Allah ﷻ has a very unique way of teaching, reminding, and training those close to Him. That is why Allah ﷻ gently reprimanded him for his answer and revealed to him that there is a servant of his at the meeting point of the two seas (Indian Ocean and Red Sea[146]) who is more knowledgeable than him. This doesn't mean that al-Khaḍir had a higher station than Mūsa ﷺ. What it means is that he had a special field of knowledge given to him that Mūsa ﷺ didn't have and was not blessed with.

When Mūsa ﷺ learned about al-Khaḍir and his special knowledge it created this intense desire, interest, and determination to seek this knowledge. So he asked Allah ﷻ, "How can I find him?" Allah ﷻ told him to cook a fish, place it in a basket, and head towards the meeting point of the two seas. The place where you lose the fish is the place where you will find al-Khaḍir. Mūsa ﷺ set out with his servant and student Yūsha ibn Nūn, who in English is known as Joshua.[147] This is where Allah ﷻ starts the story in the Quran.

146 This is one opinion regarding the meeting point of the two seas.

147 Bukhārī, *k. al-ʿilm, b. mā yustaḥabb lī al-ʿālim idhā su'ila ayy al-nās aʿlam fayakil al-ʿilm ilā Allah,* 122

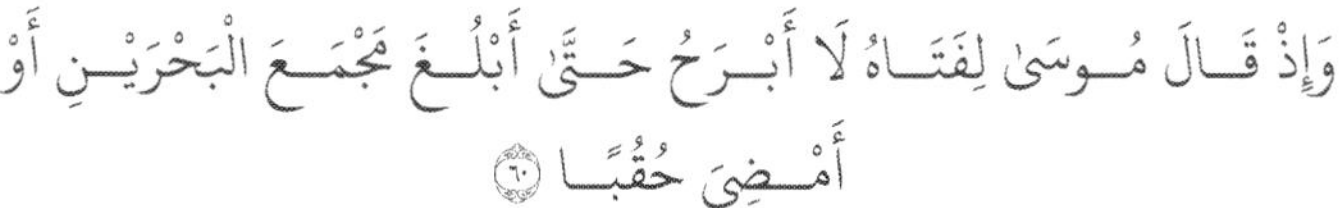

[60] And when Mūsa said to his servant, "I shall continue on till I reach the junction of the two seas, even if I journey for a long time."

In order to find al-Khaḍir, the man of God who possessed unique knowledge that was unknown to Mūsa ﷺ, he was instructed by Allah ﷻ to travel to the meeting point or junction of the two seas. As mentioned earlier, when Mūsa ﷺ learned about al-Khaḍir and his knowledge he developed this intense desire, righteous zeal, interest, and enthusiasm to seek knowledge. Mūsa ﷺ in his determination said that he would continue travelling until he reaches this junction even if it takes him a long time. "I shall continue on till I reach the junction of the two seas, even if I journey for a long time." Meaning, that he was determined to travel to this location regardless of how long it took.

There's a lot of discussion among the commentators regarding the exact location of the junction of the two seas. Some mention that it is referring to the point where the freshwater of rivers meets the salt water of the seas. Others mention that it's the meeting point between the Indian Ocean and the Red Sea, or the Persian Gulf and the Mediterranean Sea. The actual geographical location is ultimately immaterial to the story; it doesn't really matter. The narration mentions that they continued to travel until they reached a large rock where they decided to rest for a while. Both of them fell asleep. As they were sleeping, all of a sudden, their fish came to life, jumped out of the basket and into the ocean. Allah ﷻ stopped the flow of water behind the fish as it moved through the water forming a tunnel or path that Mūsa ﷺ would later follow.

فَلَمَّا بَلَغَا مَجْمَعَ بَيْنِهِمَا نَسِيَا حُوتَهُمَا فَاتَّخَذَ سَبِيلَهُۥ فِى ٱلْبَحْرِ سَرَبًا ﴿٦١﴾

[61] Then when they reached the junction of the two, they forgot their fish, and it made its way to the sea, burrowing away.

According to the narration, when Mūsa ﷺ and Yūsha arrived at the junction of the two seas they decided to take a break and rest. The narration seems to suggest that they didn't recognize this as their destination. While they were resting, Yūshā witnessed this extraordinary event of the fish stirring to life and making its way into the ocean. He saw the fish make its way into the sea, forging and forming a path. According to a narration mentioned by ibn Kathīr, as the fish swam the water behind it formed a sort of path or tunnel that Mūsa ﷺ was then able to follow.[148] Since Mūsa ﷺ was resting he didn't want to disturb him and decided to inform him of this when he woke up. When Mūsa ﷺ woke up he forgot to tell him and they continued on their journey. They traveled for another day and night. After traveling for another day and night, Mūsa ﷺ finally felt hungry.

148 ibn Kathīr, *Tafsīr al-Quran al-ʿAẓīm*, 9:162

فَلَمَّا جَاوَزَا قَالَ لِفَتَاهُ آتِنَا غَدَاءَنَا لَقَدْ لَقِينَا مِن سَفَرِنَا هَٰذَا
نَصَبًا ﴿٦٢﴾

62 Then when they had passed beyond, he said to his servant, "Bring us our meal. We have certainly met with weariness on this journey of ours."

They had passed the meeting point of the two seas, which is where they decided to rest and where the fish escaped from the basket. When Mūsa ﵇ finally felt hungry he asked Yūshā to take out the fish that they had prepared to eat saying, "Bring us our meal. We have certainly met with weariness on this journey of ours." One of the lessons we can learn from this portion of the story is that it is permissible to inform others of any inconvenience, difficulty, hardship, pain, or illness we may be experiencing. This doesn't go against the concept of being content with the decree of Allah ﷻ and accepting it. Another lesson we learn is that it is important to plan and prepare for a journey and part of that is arranging one's provisions such as food. This planning and preparation is a part of tawakkul, relying upon Allah ﷻ.

In the narration the Prophet ﷺ says, "Musa didn't feel any fatigue until he passed the place Allah ﷻ informed him of. When Mūsa ﵇ asked for food that is when Yūsha remembered what had happened to the fish."[149]

149 Qurṭubī, *al-Jāmiʿ lī Aḥkām al-Quran*, 13:321

VERSE 63

قَالَ أَرَأَيْتَ إِذْ أَوَيْنَا إِلَى الصَّخْرَةِ فَإِنِّي نَسِيتُ الْحُوتَ وَمَا أَنسَانِيهُ
إِلَّا الشَّيْطَانُ أَنْ أَذْكُرَهُ ۚ وَاتَّخَذَ سَبِيلَهُ فِي الْبَحْرِ عَجَبًا ﴿٦٣﴾

63 He said, "You see, when we took refuge at the rock, indeed I forgot the fish – and nothing made me forget to mention it except Satan – and it made its way to the sea in a wondrous manner!"

Yūsha told Mūsa that while they were resting at the rock the fish miraculously came back to life and made its way into the ocean in a wondrous manner and that he completely forgot to tell him. As an excuse he says that Satan made him forget to mention it. When Mūsa heard this he remarked,

VERSE 64

قَالَ ذَٰلِكَ مَا كُنَّا نَبْغِ ۚ فَارْتَدَّا عَلَىٰ آثَارِهِمَا قَصَصًا ﴿٦٤﴾

[64] He said, "That is what we were seeking!" So they turned back, retracing their steps.

Mūsa ﷺ immediately realized that the place where the fish was lost to the sea was exactly the place they were looking for. This is the location where he would meet the servant of Allah ﷻ more knowledgeable than him. They turned back, retracing their steps to that rock.

VERSE 65

فَوَجَدَا عَبْدًا مِّنْ عِبَادِنَا آتَيْنَاهُ رَحْمَةً مِّنْ عِندِنَا وَعَلَّمْنَاهُ مِن لَّدُنَّا عِلْمًا ﴿٦٥﴾

[65] There they found a servant from among Our servants who We had granted a mercy from Us and whom We had taught knowledge from Our presence.

When they returned to that rock they found a man lying there covered in a white sheet. Mūsa ﷺ greeted him with salām startling al-Khaḍir who replied, "Where is this salām coming from in this land? Who are you?" He replied, "Mūsa." al-Khaḍir asked, "Musa of Banī Isrā'īl?" He answered, "Yes."[150] The "servant from among our servants" is identified by all commentators as al-Khaḍir, which is translated as the Green One. It's mentioned that wherever he prayed or stood everything around him would become green. The Prophet ﷺ said, "He was named al-Khaḍir because

150 Bukhārī, *k. al-tafsīr, b. wa idh qāl Mūsa li fatāhu...*, 4725

he sat on barren land and it turned green beneath him." [151]

There's an interesting discussion among the mufassirūn (scholars of Quran interpretation) regarding his status as well; was he a prophet, a messenger, an ascetic, or simply a righteous servant of Allah? There are several theories but what we do know with absolute certainty is exactly what the Quran tells us. He was a righteous servant who was granted unique divine mercy and was given a special type of knowledge from Allah ﷻ. Some of the commentators mention that "raḥmah" is referring to the fact that he was a wali; a very devout and close servant of Allah ﷻ. The knowledge from Allah ﷻ is knowledge from the unseen that He taught to al-Khaḍir. It's an understanding of the Divine wisdom and reason behind the occurrence of certain events. It refers to an esoteric knowledge of certain realities and truths that he received from Allah ﷻ through inspiration (ilhām).

VERSE 66

قَالَ لَهُۥ مُوسَىٰ هَلْ أَتَّبِعُكَ عَلَىٰٓ أَن تُعَلِّمَنِ مِمَّا عُلِّمْتَ رُشْدًا ﴿٦٦﴾

66 Mūsa ﷺ said to him , "May I follow you, so that you can teach me some of that which you have been taught of sound judgment?"

Mūsa ﷺ asked him with the utmost respect and humility to be his student. This form of questioning, this request and the way he phrased it, is full of humility, good manners, and etiquettes. Mūsa ﷺ made himself a follower of al-Khaḍir, asked for permission to join him, and admitted his ignorance regarding the knowledge that al-Khaḍir

151 Tirmidhī, *k. tafsīr al-Quran ʿan rasūl Allah*, 3444

had. al-Khaḍir responded to his request as Allah ﷻ tells us,

VERSES 67-68

قَالَ إِنَّكَ لَن تَسْتَطِيعَ مَعِيَ صَبْرًا ﴿٦٧﴾ وَكَيْفَ تَصْبِرُ عَلَىٰ مَا لَمْ تُحِطْ بِهِ خُبْرًا ﴿٦٨﴾

[67] He said, "Truly you will not be able to bear patiently with me. [68] And how can you be patient with that which you have no knowledge?

Al-Khaḍir recognized that he would do things that Mūsa ﷺ would find to be illogical, irrational, and even impermissible. Things that on the surface level seem to be horrible and despicable. He explains to Mūsa ﷺ that he wouldn't be able to be patient with him and his actions saying, "Truly you will not be able to bear patiently with me." He also tells him one of the reasons why he knows that he won't be able to patient, "and how can you be patient with that which you have no knowledge?" How will you be patient regarding matters and affairs you are unaware of and that seem strange and illogical to you? As is mentioned in the ḥadīth recorded in Bukhārī he tells Mūsa ﷺ, "O Mūsa! I have knowledge from Allah that you don't have that He taught me. And you have some knowledge from Allah that He taught you, which I don't have." [152]

This statement foreshadows that Mūsa ﷺ and al-Khaḍir would eventually part ways. al-Khaḍir knew that Mūsa ﷺ would not be able to bear

152 Bukhārī, *k. al-ʿilm, b. mā yustaḥabb lī al-ʿālim idhā su'ila ayy al-nās aʿlam fayakil al-ʿilm ilā Allah*, 122

patiently with him. Mūsa ﵇ was a Prophet entrusted with upholding Divine Law, while al-Khaḍir had been entrusted with certain acts that outwardly seemed to violate that Divine Law.

Mūsa ﵇ is extremely eager to learn. He resolves to be patient and obedient while relying upon the will of Allah ﷻ. He says,

قَالَ سَتَجِدُنِيٓ إِن شَآءَ ٱللَّهُ صَابِرٗا وَلَآ أَعۡصِي لَكَ أَمۡرٗا ٦٩

[69] He said, "You will find me patient, if Allah wills, and I shall not disobey you in any matter."

Meaning, don't worry, you'll find me to be patient, if Allah ﷻ wills, and I won't disobey, question, or challenge you in any matter. It is very interesting to note the parallel here between the Prophet ﷺ being reminded to say "if Allah ﷻ wills" earlier in the Sūrah and Mūsa ﵇ mentioning it here highlighting that this is an important theme of the Sūrah. He's saying that he will try his best to follow and obey al-Khaḍir, but if something happens that goes against that, it is the will of Allah ﷻ. This convinced al-Khaḍir to allow Mūsa ﵇ to accompany him as his student but with certain conditions.

قَالَ فَإِنِ اتَّبَعْتَنِي فَلَا تَسْأَلْنِي عَن شَيْءٍ حَتَّىٰ أُحْدِثَ لَكَ مِنْهُ
ذِكْرًا ﴿٧٠﴾

[70] He said, "If you will follow me, then don't question me about anything until I mention it to you."

Meaning, he told Mūsa ﵇ that if you follow me on this journey and want to be my student, then you're not allowed to ask me about anything or challenge anything I do until I allow you to do so. Mūsa ﵇ accepted this condition and then they both set out on their very interesting and eventful journey together.

فَانطَلَقَا حَتَّىٰ إِذَا رَكِبَا فِي السَّفِينَةِ خَرَقَهَا ۖ قَالَ أَخَرَقْتَهَا لِتُغْرِقَ
أَهْلَهَا لَقَدْ جِئْتَ شَيْئًا إِمْرًا ﴿٧١﴾

[71] So they both went on till, when they had embarked upon

a ship, he made a hole in it. He said, "Have you made a hole in it to drown its people? Certainly you have done a grave thing."

They set out walking together along the shore, looking to hitch a ride on a ship. As they were walking, a ship passed by them and al-Khaḍir asked the crew for a ride. The sailors knew al-Khaḍir, so they let both him and Mūsa ﷺ come on board without any charge. After traveling for a while, al-Khaḍir got up and pulled out one of the planks from the bottom of the ship using an axe, making a hole in it.[153] This seemingly careless and dangerous act placed everyone on the ship in danger of drowning. Obviously this seemingly absurd, ungrateful, and cruel behavior surprised Mūsa ﷺ. He was literally in shock. He couldn't understand why al-Khaḍir would do such a thing to the sailors who helped them out and were doing them a favor. This went against his moral compass of what's right and wrong. Mūsa ﷺ forgot about the conditions of his teacher and objected. These people did us a favor and gave us a free ride and you're pulling a plank to sink their ship? You've done something terrible. "Have you made a hole in it to drown its people? Certainly you have done a grave thing." al-Khaḍir then reminded him gently with patience about their agreement.

VERSE 72

قَالَ أَلَمْ أَقُلْ إِنَّكَ لَن تَسْتَطِيعَ مَعِيَ صَبْرًا ﴿٧٢﴾

72 He said, "Did I not say that you can never bear with me patiently?"

---

153 Bukhārī, *k. al-tafsīr, b. wa idh qāl Mūsa li fatāhu...*, 4725

Didn't I tell you that you wouldn't have the patience to deal with me and my actions? The way he says this shows that he was willing to overlook and tolerate Mūsa's ﷵ impatience. Mūsa ﷵ felt a sense of regret and apologized to al-Khaḍir telling him that he completely forgot about his deal.

قَالَ لَا تُؤَاخِذْنِي بِمَا نَسِيتُ وَلَا تُرْهِقْنِي مِنْ أَمْرِي عُسْرًا ﴿٧٣﴾

[73] He (Mūsa ﷵ) said, "Do not hold me responsible for what I forgot, and do not make my course too difficult for me."

He apologized. He said please don't hold me responsible for what I forgot and allow me to continue traveling in your company. While telling the story, the Prophet ﷺ says, "The first (question) was out of forgetfulness. While this conversation was taking place a bird came and sat on the side of the boat and took a sip of water from the ocean. al-Khaḍir said to Mūsa ﷵ, 'My knowledge and yours combined in comparison to the knowledge of Allah ﷻ is like the sip of water compared to the ocean.'"[154] al-Khaḍir accepted his apology and they continued traveling on their way.

---

154 Bukhārī, *k. al-tafsīr, b. wa idh qāl Mūsa li fatāhu lā abraḥu ḥatta ablugha majmaʿ al-baḥrain aw amḍiya ḥuquban,* 4725

VERSE 74

فَانطَلَقَا حَتَّىٰٓ إِذَا لَقِيَا غُلَٰمًا فَقَتَلَهُۥ قَالَ أَقَتَلْتَ نَفْسًا زَكِيَّةً
بِغَيْرِ نَفْسٍ لَّقَدْ جِئْتَ شَيْـًٔا نُّكْرًا ﴿٧٤﴾

74 So, they moved ahead until when they met a boy, he killed him (the boy). He (Musa ﷺ) said, "Did you kill an innocent soul while he did not kill anyone? You have committed a heinous act indeed."

"So they continued..." They both got off the ship and started walking along the shore until they came across a young boy playing with his friends. al-Khaḍir went up to this young boy and killed him by either strangling him to death or striking him on his head.[155] This was just way too much for Mūsa ﷺ to handle. He objected even more vehemently. How can he kill an innocent young child for no reason whatsoever? To Mūsa ﷺ this seemed absolutely absurd, cruel, cold-hearted, evil, and unjustified. It was too much for him to tolerate patiently despite his promise not to question anything that he saw. So he said, "How can you kill a pure innocent child for no reason whatsoever? You have done something unjustified and have committed a heinous act." Once again al-Khaḍir reminds him of the condition that he made and the promise that Mūsa ﷺ had given.

155 Bukhārī, *k. al-tafsīr, b. wa idh qāl Mūsa li fatāhu...*, 4725

VERSE 75

قَالَ أَلَمْ أَقُل لَّكَ إِنَّكَ لَن تَسْتَطِيعَ مَعِىَ صَبْرًا ﴿٧٥﴾

[75] He said, "Did I not tell you that you can never bear with me patiently?"

Didn't I warn you that you wouldn't be able to handle what I would do? Didn't I tell you that you wouldn't be able to remain silent when I do certain things? Didn't I tell you that you would not be able to patiently observe some of the things I would do? In this reminder, al-Khaḍir added the word "laka (you)" to show that this time his reminder is more severe and clear. The first time someone forgets and makes a mistake it's overlooked. The second time it's also overlooked but with a sense of hesitation. Mūsa عليه السلام again feels a sense of regret for breaking his word and not sticking to the conditions of al-Khaḍir. He's now done this twice, so he apologizes by saying,

VERSE 76

قَالَ إِن سَأَلْتُكَ عَن شَىْءٍۭ بَعْدَهَا فَلَا تُصَاحِبْنِى ۖ قَدْ بَلَغْتَ مِن

لَّدُنِّي عُذْرًا ﴿٧٦﴾

[76] He said, "If I ask you about something after this, do not keep me in your company. You have had enough excuses from me."

Mūsa apologizes once again for questioning al-Khaḍir, but this time gives himself one last chance. He says that if he questions al-Khaḍir one more time, then al-Khaḍir can choose to part ways with him. He stipulated this condition upon himself. Once again al-Khaḍir accepts his apology and they set off on their way. After commenting on this part, ibn Kathīr narrates a ḥadīth from the Prophet. He writes, "ibn Jarīr narrated from ibn Abbās that Ubayy ibn Kab said that whenever the Prophet mentioned anyone, he would pray for himself first. One day he said, 'May the mercy of Allah be upon us and upon Mūsa. If he had stayed with his companion he would have seen wonders, but he said, 'If I ask you about something after this, do not keep me in your company. You have had enough excuses from me'.'"[156] This brings us to the third and last adventure they had together.

VERSE 77

فَانطَلَقَا حَتَّىٰٓ إِذَآ أَتَيَآ أَهْلَ قَرْيَةٍ اسْتَطْعَمَآ أَهْلَهَا فَأَبَوْا۟ أَن يُضَيِّفُوهُمَا فَوَجَدَا فِيهَا جِدَارًا يُرِيدُ أَن يَنقَضَّ فَأَقَامَهُۥ قَالَ لَوْ شِئْتَ لَتَّخَذْتَ عَلَيْهِ أَجْرًا ﴿٧٧﴾

156 Muslim, *k. al-faḍā'il, b. min faḍā'il al-khaḍir*, 2380

77 Then, they moved on until they came to the people of a town and sought food from them. But they refused to show them any hospitality. Then, they found a wall that was about to fall down. So he (al-Khaḍir) set it right. He (Mūsa) said, "If you wished, you could have charged a fee for this."

Mūsa ﷺ and al-Khaḍir continued traveling until they came upon the people of a town that most commentators identify as the ancient city of Antioch.[157] Being tired and hungry, they asked them for some food, but they refused to give them any or show them any hospitality whatsoever. As they were leaving the city, they came across a wall that was about to fall down. al-Khaḍir stopped by it and repaired it. Now this situation is also bizarre; al-Khaḍir is a complete stranger in a town that refused to give them food or host them, yet he still stops and fixes their wall for nothing in return. Mūsa ﷺ finds the situation full of irony. Why should a stranger exert so much effort in rebuilding a wall in a town where they were denied even a little food and all hospitality? He should have at least demanded some money for his labor and then they could have bought some food to eat. Mūsa ﷺ couldn't hold himself so he objected, "If you wished, you could have charged a fee for this." And that was the end of their journey together. al-Khaḍir responded,

157 Others mention that it may be the city of Eilat, al-Andalus, or somewhere in Azerbaijan. As mentioned earlier, this finer detail is irrelevant to the main purpose and moral of the story.

VERSE 78

قَالَ هَٰذَا فِرَاقُ بَيْنِي وَبَيْنِكَ ۚ سَأُنَبِّئُكَ بِتَأْوِيلِ مَا لَمْ تَسْتَطِع
عَّلَيْهِ صَبْرًا ﴿٧٨﴾

[78] He said, "This is the parting between me and you. I shall inform you of the meaning of that which you were unable to bear with patiently."

Meaning, this is the end of our relationship and this is where we'll part ways. But, before we go our separate ways, I'll explain to you the reason, wisdom, and hidden meaning behind everything I did. Up till this point in the story we've probably been just as impatient as Mūsa ﷺ; we have no clue why al-Khaḍir did all of these seemingly objectionable things. He himself explains everything in detail; why he pulled a plank out of the bottom of the ship, why he killed an innocent child, and why he rebuilt the wall without taking anything in return.

VERSE 79

أَمَّا السَّفِينَةُ فَكَانَتْ لِمَسَاكِينَ يَعْمَلُونَ فِي الْبَحْرِ فَأَرَدتُّ أَنْ

أَعِيبَهَا وَكَانَ وَرَاءَهُم مَّلِكٌ يَأْخُذُ كُلَّ سَفِينَةٍ غَصْبًا ﴿٧٩﴾

79 As for the ship, it belonged to some poor people who worked at sea. I wanted to damage it, for just beyond them was a king who was seizing every ship by force.

Al-Khaḍir is explaining that his act of damaging the ship was in reality a means of saving it and protecting the poor sailors. It is mentioned in a narration that these poor sailors were ten brothers; five of them were handicapped, while the other five worked.[158] The ship was their only source of income. They were traveling through waters controlled by a cruel, tyrannical king who would unjustly seize ships by force. al-Khaḍir says he damaged it so that they king would not take it. The damage done to the ship made it undesirable for the king and ultimately saved it for its owners. Had it been seaworthy and free from any defects, the tyrannical king would have confiscated it. By slightly damaging the ship, al-Khaḍir actually saved it; he employed a lesser harm to prevent a greater harm. Outwardly it may have seemed like damaging the ship was cruel and unjust, but in reality it was an act of kindness and generosity. Damaging the ship actually turned out to be a good thing.

VERSES 80-81

وَأَمَّا الْغُلَامُ فَكَانَ أَبَوَاهُ مُؤْمِنَيْنِ فَخَشِينَا أَن يُرْهِقَهُمَا طُغْيَانًا
وَكُفْرًا ﴿٨٠﴾ فَأَرَدْنَا أَن يُبْدِلَهُمَا رَبُّهُمَا خَيْرًا مِّنْهُ زَكَاةً وَأَقْرَبَ رُحْمًا ﴿٨١﴾

158 Qurṭubī, *al-Jāmiʿ fī Aḥkām al-Quran*, 11:34

81 And as for the young boy, his parents were believers and we feared that he would make them suffer much through rebellion and disbelief. 82 So we desired that their Lord give them in exchange one who is better than him in purity, and nearer to mercy.

Although the young child seemed to be pure and innocent, in reality the seeds of disbelief and wickedness were entrenched in his heart. As al-Khaḍir says in the ḥadīth recorded in Ṣaḥīḥ Muslim, "He was decreed to be a non-believer."[159] If he had grown up, he would have been a source of grief, worry, sadness, pain, and sorrow for his parents who were righteous believers. Their love for this child would have led them towards evil and wickedness as well. They would suffer because of their child's rebellion and disbelief. Allah ﷻ told al-Khaḍir to kill this boy to spare them that grief and that He ﷻ would replace him with a child that would be better and more dutiful. Obviously, the parents weren't aware of this at that time so to them this was a huge loss and tragedy. They weren't aware of the future difficulties that they were saved and protected from by his death.

Qatādah said, "His parents rejoiced when he was born and grieved for him when he was killed. If he had stayed alive, he would have been the cause of their doom. So let a man be content with the decree of Allah ﷻ, for the decree of Allah ﷻ for the believer, if he dislikes it, is better for him than if He were to decree something that he likes for him."[160] That's why in connection to these verses ibn Kathīr quotes the hadīth, "Allah does not decree anything for a believer, save that it is better for him."[161]

«لَا يَقْضِي اللهُ لِلْمُؤْمِنِ مِنْ قَضَاءٍ إِلَّا كَانَ خَيْرًا لَهُ»

"So we desired that their Lord give them in exchange one who is better than him in purity, and nearer to mercy." It is mentioned in a narration that the parents were blessed with a pious daughter who gave birth to a prophet who became the source of guidance and salvation for many others. So the

159 Muslim, *k. al-faḍā'il, b. min faḍā'il al-khaḍir*, 2380

160 Bayhaqī, *Shuʿab al-Īmān*, 10172

161 ibn Kathīr, *Tafsīr al-Quran al-ʿAẓīm*, 9:176

murder of this child actually turned out to be something good in the long run.

VERSE 82

وَأَمَّا الْجِدَارُ فَكَانَ لِغُلَامَيْنِ يَتِيمَيْنِ فِي الْمَدِينَةِ وَكَانَ تَحْتَهُ
كَنزٌ لَّهُمَا وَكَانَ أَبُوهُمَا صَالِحًا فَأَرَادَ رَبُّكَ أَن يَبْلُغَا أَشُدَّهُمَا
وَيَسْتَخْرِجَا كَنزَهُمَا رَحْمَةً مِّن رَّبِّكَ ۚ وَمَا فَعَلْتُهُ عَنْ أَمْرِي ۚ
ذَٰلِكَ تَأْوِيلُ مَا لَمْ تَسْطِع عَّلَيْهِ صَبْرًا ﴿٨٢﴾

[82] And as for the wall, it belonged to two orphan boys in the city, and beneath it was a treasure belonging to them. Their father was righteous, and your Lord desired that they should reach their maturity and extract their treasure, as a mercy from your Lord. And I didn't do this upon my own command. This is the meaning of that which you couldn't bear with patiently.

Al-Khaḍir explained to Mūsa that the wall that was about to fall that he rebuilt was covering a treasure that belonged to two orphan boys. If the wall had fallen down, the treasure would have been exposed, the people of the town would have taken it unjustly, and the orphan children would have been deprived of their wealth. By rebuilding the wall, al-Khaḍir made it possible for them to access their treasure when they grew up. This was done partially because their father was a righteous and pious man. ibn Abbās mentions that the "treasure" was knowledge written on some parchment. It read, "With the name of Allah the Most Merciful the Very Merciful. I'm amazed by a person who believes in the Divine Decree of Allah, how can they be sad? I'm amazed by the one who believes in [the concept of] rizq/provision, how can they labor away? I'm amazed by the one who believes in death, how can they be joyous? I'm amazed by the one who believes in Judgment, how can they be unmindful? I'm amazed by the one who believes in this world and its temporary nature, how can they be content with it? There's no deity worthy of worship except Allah and Muḥammad is the Messenger of Allah."[162]

al-Khaḍir then explains to Mūsa ﷺ that he didn't do any of these things based on his own accord or understanding. Rather, he did them according to the Divine command, decree, and will of Allah ﷻ. "And I didn't do this upon my own command." He concludes by saying, "This is the meaning of that which you couldn't bear with patiently." Meaning, this is the explanation of my actions that you didn't understand and weren't able to be patient with.

KEY LESSONS FROM THE STORY OF MŪSA عليه السلام AND AL-KHAḌIR

There are several important lessons, morals, and reminders that we can learn and derive from this very interesting and unique story.

1.

Intellectual humility – Our knowledge regarding a specific topic or subject, our understanding of a certain issue, or our expertise in a certain field, shouldn't make us proud and arrogant. It shouldn't make us think that we're better than anyone else. Rather it should make us humble; it should create a sense of gratitude and humility. We should express gratitude to the One who gave us that knowledge and should recognize that there's much more that we don't know. And that's the lesson that Allah ﷻ taught Mūsa ﷺ. When he was asked who is the most knowledgeable individual, Mūsa ﷺ, based on his

162 Qurṭubī, *al-Jāmiʿ fī Aḥkām al-Quran*, 13:355

own understanding and station as a prophet, assumed that he was. So Allah ﷻ gently reprimanded him for his answer and revealed to him that there is a servant of his at the meeting point of the two seas (Indian Ocean and Red Sea) who is more knowledgeable than him.

No matter how advanced we become as human beings, no matter how many discoveries we make and how many inventions we create, our knowledge is still limited; it's nothing compared to the infinite knowledge of Allah ﷻ. As Allah ﷻ tells us in Sūrah Yūsuf, "Over every possessor of knowledge is one [more] knowing."[163] Similarly, in one of the narrations referenced above, al-Khaḍir tells Mūsa ﷷ, "My knowledge or your knowledge compared with the knowledge of Allah ﷻ is nothing but the small amount of water the sparrow takes in its beak."[164] This is especially true for religious knowledge; the more we learn the more we should recognize that we don't know. That's why it's important for us to not reject or disregard things that we don't know or haven't heard of. Just because we don't know something, haven't heard something, or haven't read something, doesn't mean that it doesn't exist.

Under this point also falls the importance of learning how to say "I don't know." There are several statements and incidents of scholars from the past about having the humility and intelligence to say "I don't know."

2.

The importance of seeking knowledge - Seeking knowledge is something that has to be done actively; it's not a passive activity. Knowledge isn't something that's going to come to us automatically. It's something that requires us to put in work; it requires passion, zeal, time, effort, wealth, hard work, and sacrifice. In order to seek knowledge we'll have to go through some difficulties.

Seeking knowledge is a religious obligation upon us just like praying, fasting, paying zakah and performing hajj. The Prophet ﷺ told us, "Seeking knowledge is an obligation upon every Muslim."[165] All the commentators agree that this is referring to knowledge that brings one closer to Allah ﷻ and increases their love for the Prophet ﷺ; knowledge of the Quran and Sunnah.

---

163 12:76 وَفَوْقَ كُلِّ ذِى عِلْمٍ عَلِيمٌ

164 Bukhārī, *k. al-ʿilm, b. mā wustaḥabb li al-ʿālim idhā suʾil ayy al-nās aʿlam fayakil al-ʿilm ilā Allāh*, 122

165 Ibn Mājah, *al-Muqaddimah*, 224

That's why there are so many narrations from the Prophet ﷺ that encourage us to seek knowledge. There are several aḥādīth that describe the virtues, rewards, and blessings associated with seeking knowledge. These narrations are designed to create a sense of zeal, motivation, and enthusiasm for spending time, energy, and effort in the pursuit of knowledge. The Prophet ﷺ says, "Whoever follows a path in the pursuit of knowledge, Allah will make easy for him a path to Paradise. The angels lower their wings in approval of the seeker of knowledge, and everyone in the heavens and on earth prays for forgiveness for the seeker of knowledge, even the fish in the sea. The superiority of the scholar over the worshipper is like the superiority of the moon above all other heavenly bodies. The scholars are the heirs of the Prophets, for the Prophets did not leave behind dinars or dirhams, rather they left behind knowledge, so whoever takes it has taken a great share." [166]

Interestingly, this is the only story in the Quran that talks about seeking knowledge and in it the student is required to go and look for the teacher. On a side note, the amount of knowledge we learn regarding our religion at homes or at Sunday schools is not enough. We need to have a systemized way of learning the fundamentals of our faith and religion and teaching it to our children.

3.

Respecting people of knowledge - This is another very important lesson we learn from this particular part of the story. Mūsa ﷺ is a prophet, he's Kalīm Allah, the one who spoke directly with Allah ﷻ, yet he still treated al-Khaḍir with the utmost honor and respect. Knowledge itself has a very special status in Islam and because of its status those who seek it and possess it have also been granted a special status. As the Prophet ﷺ told us, "The scholars are the heirs of the Prophets."[167] Humility is an essential characteristic that we as students must have to truly benefit from our teachers. We see this humility in the famous ḥadīth of Jibrīl ﷺ when he came in the form of a man and asked the Prophet ﷺ about Īmān, Islam, and Iḥsān. When the Companions used to sit with the Messenger of Allah ﷺ they wouldn't raise their heads out of humility, respect, and reverence. Anas ﷺ narrates, "If the Messenger of Allah ﷺ used to enter the masjid, none of us used to raise our

---

166 Ibn Mājah, *al-Muqaddimah*, 223

167 Ibn Mājah, *al-Muqaddimah*, 223

heads except Abū Bakr and Umar. They used to smile at him and he used to smile at them." It is also reported on the authority of Ubādah ibn al-Ṣāmit ﷺ that the Messenger of Allah ﷺ said regarding respecting scholars and honoring them, "He is not from my community who does not venerate our elders, have mercy on our youth, and know the rights of our scholars."

Disrespect of scholars and people of knowledge is a problem within our communities and has been for some time. People of the past used to say that the flesh of scholars is poisonous and the way of Allah ﷻ with those who insult them is well-known. Whoever insults a scholar of this Ummah with his tongue, Allah ﷻ will afflict him in this world with the death of his heart.

4.

Studying is an honorable act, but it's not the goal in and of itself. The goal is to attain guidance, insight, and to internalize Islamic values and principles such as humility, patience, forbearance, sincerity, taqwā, and tawakkul. Knowledge is meant to be transformative. Within our tradition, learning is not simply an academic endeavor; it is not done simply to acquire information. The purpose of knowledge is to internalize it and act upon it so that we can draw nearer to our Lord and Creator. Beneficial knowledge is the knowledge that translates into action, increasing one's love for Allah ﷻ and His Messenger ﷺ.

5.

One of the most powerful and profound lessons we learn from this entire episode is that oftentimes a tragedy is a blessing in disguise. Everything that happens in this world, whether good or bad, happens according to the Divine will and decree of Allah ﷻ. There's some deep divine wisdom behind every single thing that happens in this world. When something good happens we recognize it as a blessing. For example, if we get a good job, get a raise at work, purchase a new car, or are blessed with the birth of a child, we recognize these as amazing favors from Allah ﷻ. On the other hand, whenever we face set-backs, difficulties, hardships, challenges, and tragedies we tend to lose patience.

This incident is teaching us that difficulties, tests, trials, challenges, and hardships are oftentimes blessing in disguise. The first thing to understand is that Allah ﷻ isn't sending these difficulties our way to break us or destroy us. Rather He's sending them our way to test our patience, strength, endurance, and faith; as a source of mercy and a reminder. As a way of nurturing and training us to be the best version of ourselves. He ﷻ is reminding us to turn back to Him, to hold on to our faith, to be steadfast, patient, strong, and to persevere.

When we're struggling and going through difficult times we shouldn't assume that somehow Allah ﷻ is displeased with us. Similarly, when we're comfortable and enjoying life we shouldn't assume that Allah ﷻ is pleased with us. The opposite can be true. The Prophet ﷺ said, "If Allah ﷻ wants good for his servant, He hurries on his punishment in this world, and if He wills ill for a servant, He holds back punishing him for his sin so He can give it to him in full on the Day of Resurrection."[168] Every difficulty we experience in this world is actually a source of blessing for us. The Prophet ﷺ said, "No fatigue, illness, anxiety, sorrow, harm, or sadness afflicts any Muslim, even to the extent of a thorn pricking him, without Allah wiping out his sins by it."[169]

Allah ﷻ tells us that the main tool, the key to deal with the world and all the problems it contains, is through patience and turning towards Him. When we're dealing with our problems we should turn to Allah ﷻ seeking His help, aid, assistance, and support. We should engage in dhikr, read Quran, spend time in prayer and reflection, and try to be around good company. We should try to focus our attention, our spiritual and emotional energy on our relationship with Allah ﷻ instead of our problem. By doing so we'll find peace and comfort and true contentment.

Part of patience is recognizing that whatever we're going through is something that we can handle and that whatever we're experiencing will not last forever. That's why throughout the Quran whenever Allah ﷻ consoles and comforts the Prophet ﷺ, He reminds him to be patient and to turn to him. "So be patient over what they say and exalt [Allah] with praise of your Lord."[170] "So be patient. Indeed, the promise of Allah is truth."[171] "So be ptient, [O Muḥammad], over what they say and exalt [Allah] with praise of your Lord

168 Tirmidhī, *k. al-Zuhd ʿan Rasūlillah, b. mā jā'a fī al-ṣabr ʿalā al-balā'a*, 2396

169 Bukhārī, *k. al-Marḍā, b. Mā jā'a fī kaffārah al-maraḍ*, 5641

170 20.130 فَاصْبِرْ عَلَى مَا يَقُولُونَ وَسَبِّحْ بِحَمْدِ رَبِّكَ

171 30:60 فَاصْبِرْ إِنَّ وَعْدَ اللَّهِ حَقٌّ

before the rising of the sun and before its setting."[172]

6.

Being content with the Divine decree of Allah ﷻ - Having faith in the decree of Allah ﷻ and His pre-knowledge is one of the most fundamental aspects of faith; it is an integral part of īmān. Every single thing that happens in this world, both the good and the bad, based on our limited perception, happens according to the Divine will, decree, plan, and wisdom of Allah ﷻ. Allah ﷻ tells us, "Misfortunes can only happen with God's permission—He will guide the heart of anyone who believes in Him: God knows all things."[173]

It is our responsibility as believers to be content with the will and decree of Allah ﷻ. The attitude we are supposed to have when afflicted with these difficulties is to recognize that they are from Allah ﷻ. As Allah ﷻ mentions in Sūrah al-Baqarah, "Those who say, when afflicted with a calamity, 'We belong to God and to Him we shall return.'"[174] Part of being content with Allah's decree is to internalize the reality that everything that happens in this world has some deep divine wisdom behind it. Sometimes we may recognize what that wisdom is, and oftentimes we will not.

7.

Patience - Ṣabr is usually translated as patience. However, this translation is underinclusive. Part of ṣabr is definitely patience; however, it also includes forbearance, strength, discipline, self-restraint, and being content with the decree of Allah ﷻ. That is why the scholars mention that there are three types of ṣabr:

1. al-ṣabr alā al-ṭāat (ṣabr upon acts of obedience),
2. al-ṣabr an al-maāṣī (ṣabr against acts of disobedience), and
3. al-ṣabr alā aqdārillah (ṣabr with the decree of Allah)

It takes ṣabr in the form of discipline to obey the commandments of Allah ﷻ such as praying and fasting. It requires ṣabr in the form of self-restraint and self-control to stay away from His prohibitions. It also requires

---

172 50:39 فَاصْبِرْ عَلَىٰ مَا يَقُولُونَ وَسَبِّحْ بِحَمْدِ رَبِّكَ قَبْلَ طُلُوعِ الشَّمْسِ وَقَبْلَ الْغُرُوبِ

173 64:11 مَا أَصَابَ مِن مُّصِيبَةٍ إِلَّا بِإِذْنِ اللَّهِ ۗ وَمَن يُؤْمِن بِاللَّهِ يَهْدِ قَلْبَهُ ۚ وَاللَّهُ بِكُلِّ شَيْءٍ عَلِيمٌ

174 2:156 الَّذِينَ إِذَا أَصَابَتْهُم مُّصِيبَةٌ قَالُوا إِنَّا لِلَّهِ وَإِنَّا إِلَيْهِ رَاجِعُونَ

ṣabr in the form of patience, perseverance, and strength when dealing with difficulties and hardships.

8.

Blessing of Righteous Parents - Although every single one of us is ultimately responsible for our own decisions, there is an aspect of benefitting from the blessings and supplications of the righteous. Pious and righteous parents can have a profound and powerful impact upon their children through modeling good character, and educuating and nurturing them in the light of Divine guidance.

9.

Determination - We are encouraged to have high aspirations and work towards them with resolve and determination.

In this next set of verses, Allah ﷻ tells us the story of Dhū al-Qarnayn, a just and righteous king, who ruled over the entire known world of his time. He was a righteous servant of Allah ﷻ, who was blessed with might, power,

and sovereignty over the world along with knowledge and wisdom. He was a special servant of Allah ﷻ. We're told about his journeys to the east, west, and north as well as his building of a huge wall to prevent Ya'jūj and Ma'jūj from escaping. This narrative is the answer to the third question that the Quraysh asked the Prophet ﷺ after consulting with the Jews of Madinah. This is the fourth story mentioned in the Sūrah after the story of the people of the cave, the owner of the two gardens, and the story of Mūsa (as) and al-Khaḍir. Allah ﷻ introduces the story saying,

VERSE 83

وَيَسْـَٔلُونَكَ عَن ذِى ٱلْقَرْنَيْنِ ۖ قُلْ سَأَتْلُوا۟ عَلَيْكُم مِّنْهُ ذِكْرًا ﴿٨٣﴾

[83] They ask you about Dhū al-Qarnayn. Say, "I shall now recite to you an account of him."

Meaning, the Quraysh asked you about Dhū al-Qarnayn, after consulting with the Jews of Madinah, so tell them you will now recite some of his story to them that will answer their question.

The Quran doesn't tell us the exact identity of Dhū al-Qarnayn, why he was given that name, what time period he lived in, or the exact location of his travels and rule. All these details are extra, unnecessary and immaterial; no aspect of our belief or action depends on knowing these details. However, the commentators do get into discussions regarding these details in an attempt to present historical facts.

Some historical narratives mention that there were four people who ruled over the entire known world of their respective times, two believers and two non-believers. The two believers are Sulaymān ﷺ, the son of Dāwūd ﷺ, and Dhū al-Qarnayn. The two non-believers are Nimrūdh and Bukhtanaṣr.[175] Throughout history there have been a few people who were given the title Dhū al-Qarnayn and interestingly they all had the title Alexander as well. Some scholars held the opinion that the Dhūl al-Qarnayn mentioned in the Quran is the famous Alexander the Great, the Greek who had Aristotle as his teacher. Although he fits the description of having ruled the East and the West, he can't be the Dhū al-Qarnayn mentioned in the Quran because he was a non-believer. This is the conclusion of ibn Kathīr ﷺ.

According to ibn Kathīr ﷺ, Dhū al-Qarnayn lived during the time period of Ibrāhīm ﷺ and he also mentions that al-Khaḍir was his minister. Other researchers are of the opinion that the Dhū al-Qarnayn mentioned in the Quran is the ancient Persian king, Cyrus the Great. In modern times this theory has been given more weight because of supporting evidence. As for the name Dhū al-Qarnayn it literally means "the person with two horns." The name is due to his having reached the two 'horns' of the Sun, east and west, where it rises and where it sets during his journey. Others mentioned that he was given this title because he had a helmet or some sort of headdress with two horns or that he used to style his hair in two braids. The following is what the Quran tells us about him.

175 Qurṭubī, *al-Jāmiʿ li Aḥkām al-Quran*, 13:367

VERSE 84

إِنَّا مَكَّنَّا لَهُۥ فِي ٱلْأَرْضِ وَآتَيْنَاهُ مِن كُلِّ شَيْءٍ سَبَبًا ﴿٨٤﴾

[84] Surely, We gave him power on earth and gave him means to (have) everything (he needs).

Allah ﷻ blessed and favored him with all the material tools, resources, knowledge, insight, qualities, and experience needed to be an effective and just ruler. Allah ﷻ gave him everything he needed to maintain just rule, establish peace, and extend his area of influence. This is a very important point to note; Allah ﷻ alone is the One who granted him the ability to rule over the known world of his time. It had nothing to do with his own abilities or capabilities.

VERSES 85-86

فَأَتْبَعَ سَبَبًا ﴿٨٥﴾ حَتَّىٰٓ إِذَا بَلَغَ مَغْرِبَ ٱلشَّمْسِ وَجَدَهَا تَغْرُبُ
فِي عَيْنٍ حَمِئَةٍ وَوَجَدَ عِندَهَا قَوْمًا ۗ قُلْنَا يَا ذَا ٱلْقَرْنَيْنِ إِمَّا أَن
تُعَذِّبَ وَإِمَّا أَن تَتَّخِذَ فِيهِمْ حُسْنًا ﴿٨٦﴾

> [85] So he followed a course, [86] until when he reached the point of sunset, he found it setting into a murky spring, and found a people near it. We said, "O Dhū al-Qarnayn, either punish them or treat them well."

He traveled towards the West until he reached a particular location where the sun sets. Geographically it is described as a location to the extreme west beyond which there was only an Ocean, which was most likely the Atlantic. There he found the sun setting into a dark, muddy spring, meaning that it looked as if the sun were setting into the Sea. Depending on your geographic location, the sun seems to set into different places within the horizon. For example, from our perspective sometimes it looks like the sun is setting into the ocean, or behind a mountain, or into the sand.

At this location he came across a nation of non-believers. Allah ﷻ told him through ilhām (inspiration) that he has a choice; he can either punish them for their disbelief or he could deal with them kindly, invite them to the truth, and teach them about submission to Allah ﷻ. After inviting them towards the truth, he could then reward those who believed and punish those who chose to disbelieve. He chose to invite them to belief first and then reward the believers and punish the non-believers.

قَالَ أَمَّا مَن ظَلَمَ فَسَوْفَ نُعَذِّبُهُۥ ثُمَّ يُرَدُّ إِلَىٰ رَبِّهِۦ فَيُعَذِّبُهُۥ عَذَابًا
نُّكْرًا ﴿٨٧﴾ وَأَمَّا مَنْ ءَامَنَ وَعَمِلَ صَٰلِحًا فَلَهُۥ جَزَآءً ٱلْحُسْنَىٰ ۖ
وَسَنَقُولُ لَهُۥ مِنْ أَمْرِنَا يُسْرًا ﴿٨٨﴾

> 87 He said, "As for him who does wrong, we shall punish him, then he will be sent back to his Lord, and He will punish him with a severe punishment. 88 As for the one who believes and acts righteously, he will have the best (life) as reward, and we shall speak to him politely in our directions."

In these verses, Allah ﷻ is highlighting an expression of Dhū al-Qarnayn's justice. Dhū al-Qarnayn was a just ruler who ruled according to the dictates of faith, belief, justice, fairness, and righteousness. He decided that those who were presented with the truth, Islam, and then chose to consciously reject it would be punished in this world and then Allah ﷻ will punish them in the next. They are described as those who do wrong because they wronged themselves by choosing to reject the truth, which leads to moral decay.

As for those who believe - who affirm faith in Allah ﷻ, His Prophets, the Last Day, and do righteous deeds submitting to Allah ﷻ - Dhū al-Qarnayn decided and ruled that they will be rewarded. They will be rewarded by Allah ﷻ both in this life and the next. Syed Quṭb ؒ writes, "When those who do well in the community, pursuing a fair line of action in all their pursuits, receive a good reward for their actions, and when the unjust and oppressors receive a fair punishment and humiliation, then the whole community is motivated to follow the line of goodness. But when matters go wrong, and the unjust, oppressor and corrupt people are the ones who enjoy favor with the ruler, while those who are good and fair are persecuted, then the ruler's power becomes no more than a tool of corruption and misery for the whole community. Nothing remains fair. The whole society sinks into chaos."[176] Dhū al-Qarnayn established peace and justice in this location and then decided to carry on and travel towards the East.

---

176 Quṭb, *fī Ẓilāl al-Quran*, 4:2291

ثُمَّ أَتْبَعَ سَبَبًا ﴿٨٩﴾ حَتَّىٰٓ إِذَا بَلَغَ مَطْلِعَ ٱلشَّمْسِ وَجَدَهَا تَطْلُعُ
عَلَىٰ قَوْمٍ لَّمْ نَجْعَل لَّهُم مِّن دُونِهَا سِتْرًا ﴿٩٠﴾

[89] Thereafter, he followed a course [90] until when he reached the point of sun-rise; he found it rising over a people for whom We did not make any shelter against it.

Dhū al-Qarnayn traveled towards the East, towards the point of sunrise, where he found a group of people who were not used to the ways of advanced people; they were seemingly primitive. The point of sunrise means that according to their perspective it seemed as if the sun were rising from their horizon; that's how it appears to the human eye. They didn't have homes, shelter, or clothes to protect themselves against the sun. These people were also non-believers and he dealt with them in the same way as he did with the previous people. He employed the same policy of fairness, justice, and building a society on faith.

VERSE 91

كَذَٰلِكَ وَقَدْ أَحَطْنَا بِمَا لَدَيْهِ خُبْرًا ﴿٩١﴾

91 Thus it was, and Our knowledge fully comprehends whatever (wealth and equipment) he had with him.

Ibn Kathīr writes that the early commentators Mujāhid and al-Suddi ﵀ said, "This means that Allah knew everything about him and his army, and nothing was hidden from Him, even though they came from so many different nations and lands. For, truly nothing is hidden from Allah in the Earth and in the heaven."[177] After establishing justice and peace, he traveled towards the North.

VERSES 92-93

ثُمَّ أَتْبَعَ سَبَبًا ﴿٩٢﴾ حَتَّىٰٓ إِذَا بَلَغَ بَيْنَ ٱلسَّدَّيْنِ وَجَدَ مِن دُونِهِمَا
قَوْمًا لَّا يَكَادُونَ يَفْقَهُونَ قَوْلًا ﴿٩٣﴾

177 Ibn Kathīr, *Tafsīr al-Quran al-ʿAẓīm*, 9:190

[92] Thereafter he followed a course [93] until he reached between the two mountains, he found by them a people who were almost unable to understand anything said.

Then he traveled towards the North until he reached a point between two mountains. There he found a nation of people who were barely able to understand what he was saying because of their foreign language. They said to him through a translator or through some other means,

VERSE 94

قَالُوا يَـا ذَا الْقَرْنَـيْنِ إِنَّ يَأْجُـوجَ وَمَأْجُـوجَ مُفْسِـدُونَ فِي الْأَرْضِ فَهَلْ
نَجْعَـلُ لَـكَ خَرْجًـا عَلَىٰٓ أَن تَجْعَـلَ بَيْنَنَـا وَبَيْنَهُـمْ سَـدًّا ﴿٩٤﴾

[94] They said, "O Dhū al-Qarnayn, the (tribes of) Ya'jūj and Ma'jūj (Gog and Magog) are mischief makers on the earth. So, should we assign a payment for you on condition that you make a barrier between us and them?"

These people recognized that Dhū al-Qarnayn was a fair and just ruler so they asked him for help against the menace of Ya'jūj and Ma'jūj. Ya'jūj and Ma'jūj is the name of a tribe of people that Allah ﷻ speaks about in the Quran and that the Prophet ﷺ warns his Companions of. There's a lot of speculation regarding who exactly they are and what area or region they're from, but nothing can be said with certainty. Ya'jūj and Ma'jūj were known for their violence and plundering, and would harass these people. They complained to Dhū al-Qarnayn saying that Ya'jūj and Ma'jūj spread mischief and corruption in their lands by killing and destruction. They offered to pay Dhū al-Qarnayn some money to build a barrier to protect them and prevent Ya'jūj and Ma'jūj from reaching their town.

قَالَ مَا مَكَّنِّي فِيهِ رَبِّي خَيْرٌ فَأَعِينُونِي بِقُوَّةٍ أَجْعَلْ بَيْنَكُمْ
وَبَيْنَهُمْ رَدْمًا ﴿٩٥﴾

95 He said, "What my Lord has (already) given in my control is better (for me than the payment you are offering to me), so help me (only) with strength, and I shall make a barrier between you and them.

In simple words he told them that he didn't want or need their money, but he will need their help in constructing and building this large barrier. Allah ﷻ had given him such great wealth, intelligence, and power that he had no need for what they could offer him. This statement also highlights his humility; he attributed his power, authority, kingdom, and wealth to Allah ﷻ and not himself. He would provide this service simply for the sake of righteousness and doing good.

VERSE 96

آتُونِي زُبَرَ الْحَدِيدِ ۖ حَتَّىٰ إِذَا سَاوَىٰ بَيْنَ الصَّدَفَيْنِ قَالَ انفُخُوا ۖ
حَتَّىٰ إِذَا جَعَلَهُ نَارًا قَالَ آتُونِي أُفْرِغْ عَلَيْهِ قِطْرًا ﴿٩٦﴾

[96] Bring me big pieces of iron." (They proceeded accordingly) until when he leveled (the gap) between the two cliffs, he said, "Blow." (They complied) until when he made it (like) fire, he said, "Bring me molten copper, and I will pour it upon this."

'Bring me big pieces of iron.' (They proceeded accordingly) until when he leveled (the gap) between the two cliffs." He requested the people to bring him large pieces of iron as raw material to construct this very large barrier. They brought pieces of iron and filled the space between the two mountains with it. Once they had filled the space with these iron pieces Dhū al-Qarnayn said, "Blow." Meaning, use bellows or any other instrument to heat the iron until it is extremely hot. They followed his instructions heating the iron pieces until they became extremely hot and then poured molten copper over it making a huge solid metal structure.

VERSE 97

فَمَا اسْطَاعُوا أَن يَظْهَرُوهُ وَمَا اسْتَطَاعُوا لَهُ نَقْبًا ﴿٩٧﴾

[97] So they (Ya'jūj and Ma'jūj) were not able to climb it, nor were they able to make a hole in it.

They weren't able to climb it because of its height nor were they able to make a hole in it because of its depth and strength. According to several narrations, of which I will mention one shortly, Ya'jūj and Ma'jūj try to dig through the barrier every day, but will be unable to do so until an appointed time that has been determined by Allah ﷻ.

VERSE 98

قَالَ هَٰذَا رَحْمَةٌ مِّن رَّبِّي ۖ فَإِذَا جَاءَ وَعْدُ رَبِّي جَعَلَهُ دَكَّاءَ ۖ وَكَانَ
وَعْدُ رَبِّي حَقًّا ﴿٩٨﴾

[98] He said, "This is a mercy from my Lord. Then, when the promise of my Lord will come, He will make it leveled to

the ground. The promise of my Lord is true."

Dhū al-Qarnayn humbly acknowledges and recognizes that his ability to build such a strong and impenetrable barrier was a mercy from Allah ﷻ; it had nothing to do with his own strength or ability. This once again highlights his humility and recognition of Allah ﷻ. The "promise of my Lord" is referring to the onset of the events that will lead to the Hour; the Day of Judgment. This includes the trials of Dajjāl, Ya'jūj and Ma'jūj, and the return of 'Isa ﷺ. One of these events will be that the barrier will crumble to dust and Ya'jūj and Ma'jūj will wreak havoc across the Earth. Once their barrier is opened and they're let loose, they will descend from every elevation, attacking humanity from every single corner and angle. They will come rushing down the mountains in huge groups like waves crashing down upon the people while destroying and killing everything in sight.

There are many signs of the Day of Judgment mentioned in the Quran and aḥādīth of the Prophet ﷺ. Some of them are classified as minor and others as major. Some of them will happen further away from the Day of Judgment and others will happen very close to the Day of Judgment. For example, the Prophet ﷺ being appointed and chosen as the last and final Messenger is one of the signs that the Day of Judgment is near. As the Prophet ﷺ told us, "I and the Last Hour have been sent like this and (he while doing it) joined the forefinger with the middle finger."[178] Ḥudhaifah ؓ narrated that once the Companions were sitting together in the middle of a discussion and the Prophet ﷺ came and asked what they were talking about. They said they were talking about the Day of Resurrection. The Prophet ﷺ said, "Indeed the Hour will not come until you see ten signs before it." He mentioned the smoke, Dajjāl, the beast, the rising of the sun from the west, the return of Isā ibn Maryam ﷺ, Ya'jūj and Ma'jūj, and three sinkholes; one in the East, one in the West, and one in the Arabian Peninsula, at the end of which fire would burn forth from Yemen, and would drive people to the place of their assembly.[179]

Two of the greatest trials this Ummah will face before the Day of Resurrection are the trial of Dajjāl and the attack of Ya'jūj and Ma'jūj. Both of these are major signs of the Day of Judgment and will happen very close to each

178 Muslim, *k. al-fitan wa ashrāṭ al-sā'ah, b. qurb al-sā'ah*, 2951

179 Muslim, *k. al-fitan wa ashrāṭ al-sā'ah, b. fī al-āyāt allatī takun qabl al-sā'ah*, 2901

other. There's a very lengthy ḥadīth recorded in Ṣaḥīḥ Muslim[180] narrated by al-Nawwās ibn Samān ﷺ that gives the details of these two specific trials; meaning the trial of Dajjāl and Ya'jūj and Ma'jūj. The narration tells us about the details of the fitnah of Dajjāl; his description, how long he will stay, and how exactly he's going to test us. He will stay in this world for a period of forty days; but the first day will be equivalent to one year, the second day to one month, and the rest of the days will be normal. He will move extremely swiftly across the Earth spreading his mischief and asking people to believe in him. He will continue to misguide and test people until Isā ﷺ is sent back to this world. Isā ﷺ will search for Dajjāl until he catches up with him at the eastern gate of Ludd, located in Palestine, where he will kill him.

Allah ﷻ will then reveal to Isā ﷺ, "I have brought forth from among My creatures people against whom none will be able to fight. Take My servants safely to mount (Ṭūr)." Then Allah will send Ya'jūj and Ma'jūj, as Allah says, "And they, from every elevation, will descend."[181]

Another narration from Abū Saīd al-Khudrī ﷺ[182] describes what they will do when they descend upon the people. They will be seen coming down from the mountains like waves of people overwhelming humanity, killing and destroying everything in sight. Isā ﷺ along with his companions will take refuge on Mount Ṭūr and the other Muslims will retreat to their own cities and strongholds. They (Ya'jūj and Ma'jūj) will drink all the water of the land until some of them will pass a river and drink it dry, then those who come after them will pass by that place and will say, "There used to be water here once." Then there will be no one left except those who are in their strongholds and cities. Then one of them will say, "We have defeated the people of the earth; now the people of heaven are left." One of them will shake his spear and hurl it into the sky, and it will come back stained with blood, as a test and a trial for them.

The narration of al-Nawwās ﷺ mentioned above tells us that while this is happening, Isā ﷺ and his companions will turn to Allah ﷻ asking Him to remove their distress. Allah ﷻ will answer their prayer and send an epidemic

---

180 Muslim, *k. al-fitan wa ashrāṭ al-sāʿah, b. dhikr al-dajjāl wa ṣifatuhu wa mā maʿahu*, 2937

181 21:96 وَهُم مِّن كُلِّ حَدَبٍ يَنسِلُونَ

182 ibn Mājah, *k. al-fitan, b. fitnah al-dajjāl wa khurūj ʿIsā wa khurūj Ya'jūj wa Ma'jūj*, 4079

that will completely wipe Ya'jūj and Ma'jūj out. Allah ﷻ will send some sort of insect that will attack their necks, and in the morning they will all perish as one. Then Isā ﷺ and his companions will come down and they will not find a single spot on earth that is free from their putrefaction and stench. Isā and his companions will again beseech Allah ﷻ, and He will send birds with necks like those of Bactrian camels, and they will carry them and throw them wherever Allah wills. Allah ﷻ will then send rain continuously for forty days to cleanse and purify the earth. The earth will be washed clean until it looks like a mirror. It will be said to the earth: bring forth your fruit and restore your blessing. On that day a group of people will be able to eat from one pomegranate and seek shade under its skin, and everything will be blessed. A camel will give so much milk that it will be sufficient for a whole group of people, and a cow will give so much milk that it will be sufficient for a whole clan, and a sheep will be sufficient for an entire household. (This period of extra-ordinary peace, protection and blessings will last for forty years) At that time Allah ﷻ will send a pleasant wind which will reach beneath their armpits and will take the soul of every Muslim -- or every believer -- and there will be left only the most evil of people who will commit fornication like mules, and then the Hour will come upon them.

From other narrations, we learn that Ya'jūj and Ma'jūj have already made a hole in their wall. Zainab bint Jaḥsh ﷺ narrated that once the Prophet ﷺ woke up from sleep saying, "There is no being worthy of worship except Allah; there is destruction in store for Arabia because of turmoil which is at hand, the barrier of Ya'jūj and Ma'jūj has opened so much. And Sufyān made a sign of ten with the help of his hand (in order to indicate the width of the gap) and I said, "Allah's Messenger, will we be destroyed in spite of the fact that there would be good people amongst us?" Thereupon he ﷺ said, Of course, but only when evil predominates."[183]

In a narration recorded in Tirmidhī Abū Hurairah ﷺ narrated that the Prophet ﷺ said, "Ya'jūj and Ma'jūj continue digging through the wall built by Dhū al-Qarnayn. Every day they dig so much that they reach the farthest part of the iron wall. They're so close that light from the other side is almost visible. But at that point they stop digging and decide that they will complete the task the following day. However, Allah ﷻ makes the wall just as thick

183 Muslim, *k. al-fitan wa ashrāṭ al-sāʿah, b. iqtirāb al-fitan wa fatḥ radm Ya'jūj wa Ma'jūj*, 2880

and strong as it was before so when they come back they have to start all over again. This cycle of digging and rebuilding will continue as long as Allah ﷻ wills. Then one day when it has been decreed for them to be released they will dig all the way to the end and say, 'If Allah wills we will cross it tomorrow.' So when they return the next day they will find the wall just as they left it and break through wreaking havoc on the Earth."[184]

The Sūrah follows the story of Dhū al-Qarnayn with a scene from the Day of Judgment.

وَتَرَكْنَا بَعْضَهُمْ يَوْمَئِذٍ يَمُوجُ فِي بَعْضٍ ۖ وَنُفِخَ فِي الصُّورِ
فَجَمَعْنَاهُمْ جَمْعًا ﴿٩٩﴾

99 And We shall leave them, on that day, to surge over one another like waves. And the trumpet shall be blown, and We shall gather them together.

The first part of this verse is referring to Ya'jūj and Ma'jūj and the second part refers to resurrection, when the Angel Isrāfīl ﷺ will blow into the horn bringing all creation back to life. "On that day" is referring to the day near the end of times when Ya'jūj and Ma'jūj will break through the barrier and surge down the mountains like waves upon humanity destroying everything in their way. As Allah ﷻ tells us in Sūrah al-Anbiyā, "Until when [the dam of] Gog and Magog has been opened and they, from ev-

184 Ibn Mājah, *k. al-fitan, b. fitan al-dajjāl wa khurūj 'isā ibn maryam wa khurūj ya'jūj wa ma'jūj*, 4080

ery elevation, descend…"[185] They will wreak havoc for a period of time known to Allah ﷻ until they are later destroyed.

There will be two instances when the Trumpet will be sounded. Allah ﷻ has appointed the Angel Isrāfīl ﷺ to blow into the Trumpet and he will do so twice. The first time every single thing will be destroyed. The second time every single thing will be brought back to life. This is how the day of Resurrection will start. The Ṣūr, which is a trumpet or a horn, will be blown and all of mankind will rise from their graves and come towards the plain of judgment. Abū Saīd al-Khudrī ﷺ narrates that the Messenger of Allah ﷺ said, "How can I be comfortable when the one with the horn is holding it to his lip, his ears listening for when he will be ordered to blow, so he can blow." [186]That's what Allah ﷻ is mentioning here in this verse, "And the trumpet shall be blown, and We shall gather them together."

The Sūrah then describes a scene from the day of Judgment that's specific to the non-believers; those who received the message and consciously chose to reject it and rebel against God and His Messengers.

وَعَرَضْنَا جَهَنَّمَ يَوْمَئِذٍ لِّلْكَافِرِينَ عَرْضًا ﴿١٠٠﴾ الَّذِينَ كَانَتْ أَعْيُنُهُمْ
فِي غِطَاءٍ عَن ذِكْرِي وَكَانُوا لَا يَسْتَطِيعُونَ سَمْعًا ﴿١٠١﴾

[100] And We shall present Hell, on that Day, as an array before the non-believers, [101] those whose eyes were veiled from the remembrance of Me, and could not hear.

---

185 21:96 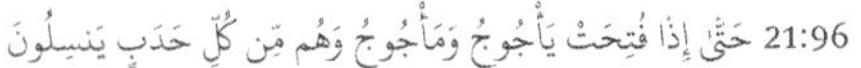

186 Tirmidhī, *k. ṣifah al-qiyāmah wa al-raqā'iq wa al-war' 'an rasūlillah*, 2618

Meaning, on the Day of Judgment Allah ﷻ will show the non-believers Hellfire, exposing it to them so that they can see it with their own eyes. They will hear its raging and frightening sounds even before entering it. Allah ﷻ then describes the non-believers with three characteristics, which are essentially three reasons why they will be punished in the hereafter. Allah ﷻ mentions the first reason as, "Those whose eyes were veiled from the remembrance of Me, and could not hear." They weren't able to understand the truth when it was presented to them because they were spiritually blind and deaf. Their faculties of seeing and hearing worked perfectly fine; however, because their hearts were corrupt and veiled in darkness they were unable to truly see and hear the message. They were blind to the signs of Allah's ﷻ existence and power all around them spread throughout the universe, so they never thought or reflected upon them. In addition to that, they weren't able to understand what was being recited to them. Meaning, they consciously chose to ignore the message and turn away from it. Here Allah ﷻ is contrasting their condition in the hereafter to their condition in the life of this world. In this world they chose to turn away from belief in the fire, but in the hereafter they won't have the option to turn away. The veil over their eyes will be removed and they will see the consequences of their choice.

أَفَحَسِبَ ٱلَّذِينَ كَفَرُوٓا۟ أَن يَتَّخِذُوا۟ عِبَادِى مِن دُونِىٓ أَوْلِيَآءَ ۚ إِنَّآ
أَعْتَدْنَا جَهَنَّمَ لِلْكَـٰفِرِينَ نُزُلًا ١٠٢

102 Do those who disbelieve reckon that they may take My servants as protectors apart from Me? Truly We have pre-

pared Hell as a welcome for the disbelievers!

Allah ﷻ is scolding them and highlighting their worst mistake and sin, which is the second reason why they will be punished. Did they really believe that they could take created beings or inanimate objects as protectors apart from Me? Did they really believe that worshipping idols, Angels, or people would benefit them or help them in any way, shape, or form? There's no help or protection except with Allah ﷻ, the One who deserves to be worshipped alone without any partners. As Allah ﷻ says in Sūrah Maryam, "No! Those "gods" will deny their worship of them and will be against them opponents [on the Day of Judgment]."[187] Allah then tells us that their punishment is Hell, which has been prepared as a resting place for them. "Truly We have prepared Hell as a welcome for the disbelievers!" The non-believers are then described as fools for thinking that their actions in this world will be of any benefit to them in the Hereafter.

VERSES 103-104

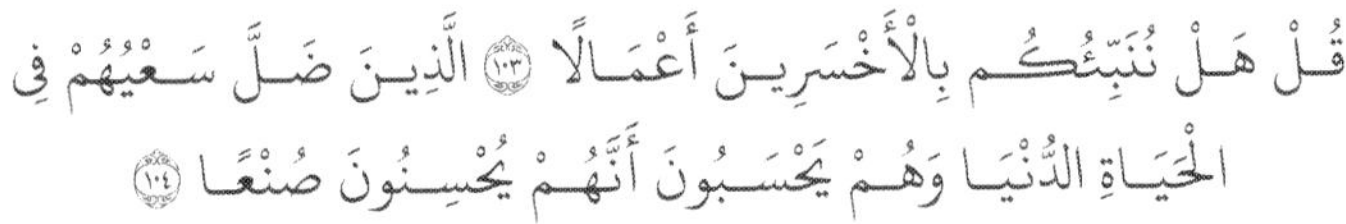

[103] Say, "Shall We inform you who are the greatest losers in respect to their deeds? [104] Those whose efforts go astray in the life of this world, while they think that they are virtuous in their works.

187 19:82 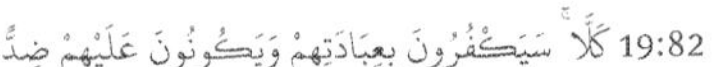

In this verse, Allah ﷻ is addressing the Prophet ﷺ directly and telling him to pose this question to the non-believers. "Shall We inform you who are the greatest losers in respect to their deeds?" Do you want to know who the greatest and biggest losers are with respect to their deeds and actions in the life of this world? They are the ones who did good deeds, put in effort, and struggled, spending time, energy, and wealth, but all of it went to waste. Those individuals who were misguided in the life of this world so their actions were guided by their wants, desires, pleasures, and corrupt beliefs. Their actions were misplaced and not guided by faith in Allah ﷻ. They think that what they are doing is virtuous and a source of reward but in reality it is all in vain. The reason why all of their efforts will go to waste is their disbelief or absence of faith.

أُولَٰئِكَ الَّذِينَ كَفَرُوا بِآيَاتِ رَبِّهِمْ وَلِقَائِهِ فَحَبِطَتْ أَعْمَالُهُمْ
فَلَا نُقِيمُ لَهُمْ يَوْمَ الْقِيَامَةِ وَزْنًا ﴿١٠٥﴾ ذَٰلِكَ جَزَاؤُهُمْ جَهَنَّمُ بِمَا
كَفَرُوا وَاتَّخَذُوا آيَاتِي وَرُسُلِي هُزُوًا ﴿١٠٦﴾

105 They are those who disbelieve in the signs of their Lord, and in the meeting with Him. So their deeds have gone to waste, and on the Day of Resurrection We shall assign them no weight. 106 That is their recompense, Hell, for having disbelieved and for having taken My signs and My Messengers in mockery.

The greatest losers with respect to their deeds are those who reject the signs of Allah ﷻ in this world; those who refuse to accept the oneness, might, power, and magnificence of Allah ﷻ, and those who refuse to believe in life after death and accountability. Their deeds will go to waste, they will not receive reward for them in the Hereafter, and on the Day of Judgment they won't have any weight. We learn from multiple verses and narrations that our deeds are going to be weighed on the Day of Judgment. If a person's good deeds outweigh their bad deeds, then they will be among the people of Paradise and if their bad deeds outweigh their good deeds then they will be in trouble. We also learn from other verses that on the Day of Judgment, it won't be about the quantity of deeds but the quality. That's why on the Day of Judgment our deeds won't be counted, but they will be weighed. It could be that the weight of one action or deed is more than a thousand other deeds because of the sincerity and excellence of the one who did it.

Those actions that are devoid of faith and sincerity will have no weight whatsoever. As Allah ﷻ says in Sūrah al-Furqān, "Then We will turn to whatever [good] deeds they did, reducing them to scattered dust."[188] Their recompense is the fire of Hell, and that is ultimate justice and fairness. They get punishment as recompense because of their rejection, disbelief, and mockery of Allah's signs and His messengers. Allah ﷻ then contrasts the punishment of the non-believers with the reward of the believers in Paradise.

VERSES 107-108

إِنَّ الَّذِينَ آمَنُوا وَعَمِلُوا الصَّالِحَاتِ كَانَتْ لَهُمْ جَنَّاتُ الْفِرْدَوْسِ نُزُلًا ﴿١٠٧﴾ خَالِدِينَ فِيهَا لَا يَبْغُونَ عَنْهَا حِوَلًا ﴿١٠٨﴾

188 25:23 وَقَدِمْنَا إِلَىٰ مَا عَمِلُوا مِنْ عَمَلٍ فَجَعَلْنَاهُ هَبَاءً مَّنثُورًا

[107] Those who believe and perform righteous deeds, theirs shall be the Gardens of Paradise as a welcome. [108] Abiding therein forever, they don't seek any change from it.

Just as Hell is a "welcome" for the non-believers, Paradise is a true "welcome" for the believers. Meaning, those who believe in the existence and oneness of Allah ﷻ, believe in the Prophet ﷺ, and life after death and that faith expresses itself through their actions, their reward will be Gardens of Paradise. Again we see this formula being mentioned; faith with righteous deeds leads to Paradise. This is the simple formula to achieve success in this world and the next. Our faith has to be real and practical; it has to translate into action. Syed Quṭb writes, "Whenever the Quran mentions reward, it precedes this by mentioning faith and good action. It is in the nature of the Islamic faith that it must never remain an idle belief that triggers no action. It must always be a living, active reality. Indeed, Islam hardly settles in a person's heart before it begins to establish itself in action and behavior. It reflects its nature and what it does to believers' consciences through its clear effects on people's lives."[189]

If we do so, then our reward will be Jannah al-Firdaws, which is the highest and most virtuous level of Paradise. The Prophet ﷺ said, "When you ask Allah for Paradise, ask Him for al-Firdaws. It is the highest level of Paradise, the middle of Paradise and the rivers of Paradise flow from it."[190] In another narration the Prophet ﷺ said, "In Paradise, there are a hundred levels, what is between every two levels is like what is between the heavens and the earth. al-Firdaws is its highest level, and from it the four rivers of Paradise are made to flow forth. So when you ask Allah, ask Him for al-Firdaws."[191]

Those who truly believe in Allah ﷻ, His Messenger ﷺ, and the Last Day and this belief leads to righteous deeds - by obeying His commandments and staying away from His prohibitions - will be rewarded with gardens of bliss. These gardens will be full of all types of pleasures; food, drink, clothes, homes, possessions, and anything else that results in joy, happiness, contentment, and bliss. They will live in it forever. The concept of eternity is

---

189 Quṭb, *fī Ẓilāl al-Quran*, 4:2296

190 Bukhārī, *k. al-jihād wa al-siyar, b. darajāt al-mujāhidīn fī sabīl Allah yuqāl hādhihi sabīlī hādhihi sabīlī*, 2790

191 ibn Mājah, k. *al-zuhd*, 4331

difficult for us as human beings to wrap our head around. We are creatures that are bound by time; we understand the concept of seconds, minutes, hours, days, weeks, months, and years. But all of these measurements and increments are finite; they are limited and will come to an end. The life of the hereafter is never ending, everlasting; it's forever. This is an extremely important reality to remember because it will help us realize and recognize that disobeying Allah ﷻ in this life, following our desires, and chasing after pleasures and comforts at the expense of salvation is just not worth it. The reward of Paradise is a promise from Allah ﷻ that will come true without a doubt. This will happen for sure without a doubt because it is the promise of Allah ﷻ and His promise always comes true. Allah ﷻ never breaks His promise.

That is a very powerful concept for us to understand. The promise of Allah ﷻ comes true without a doubt whatsoever. The question is, do we really believe the promise of Allah ﷻ? Many claim to believe in it, but do we really believe in it?

Allah ﷻ will grant them al-Firdaws as a place of welcome; a place prepared by a host to welcome, honor, and treat their guests. Imagine, Allah ﷻ the absolute Most Generous, the Most Merciful, the Very Merciful, has prepared al-Firdaws for His servants that believe and do righteous deeds. They will be in Paradise for all of eternity, enjoying all of its pleasures and not wanting or desiring anything other than it. Allah ﷻ then tells us about the extent, vastness, and limitless nature of His knowledge. He ﷻ reminds us that His knowledge is divine, infinite, and encompasses every single thing. This is also a description of the greatness and status of the Quran.

قُلْ لَوْ كَانَ الْبَحْرُ مِدَادًا لِكَلِمَاتِ رَبِّي لَنَفِدَ الْبَحْرُ قَبْلَ أَنْ تَنْفَدَ

كَلِمَاتُ رَبِّي وَلَوْ جِئْنَا بِمِثْلِهِ مَدَدًا ﴿١٠٩﴾

109 Say, "If the ocean were ink for the words of my Lord, the ocean would be exhausted before the words of my Lord were exhausted, even if We brought the like thereof to replenish it."

"The words of my Lord" may be a reference to Allah's infinite knowledge, wisdom, or the meanings of the Quran. If the oceans were turned into ink and the words of Allah ﷻ were to be written with this ink, then the ink would run out and the words of Allah ﷻ would still be left, even if more ink were to be brought. Allah ﷻ mentions a similar example in Sūrah Luqmān, "And if all trees that are on the earth were to be pens, and the ocean (converted into ink) is supported by seven seas following it, the words of Allah would not come to an end. Surely, Allah is Mighty, Wise."[192] These verses highlight the infinite knowledge, might, power, and wisdom of Allah ﷻ in a very powerful and beautiful way using extremely vivid imagery. This imagery helps us understand the vastness of Allah's knowledge, wisdom, and secrets creating a sense of awe, reverence, and humility.

The ocean is the largest and richest creation known to us as human beings. It takes up more than 70% of the surface of the Earth. We use ink to document and record our knowledge, which we think is vast and amazing. Allah ﷻ gives this example of the ocean as ink being used to write and record His words showing us that our knowledge is extremely limited. Allah ﷻ is telling us that if all the trees on the face of the Earth were turned into pens, and all the oceans into ink, and then they were used to write the words of Allah, the pens would break and the ink would finish but the knowledge of Allah ﷻ would never end. Just to provide some perspective of the sheer magnitude of what's being described, there are over three trillion trees in the world. There are over 321,003,271 cubic miles of water on the planet. That's enough water to fill 352,670,000,000,000,000,000 gallon-sized milk con-

192 31:27 وَلَوْ أَنَّمَا فِى الْأَرْضِ مِن شَجَرَةٍ أَقْلَامٌ وَالْبَحْرُ يَمُدُّهُ مِن بَعْدِهِ سَبْعَةُ أَبْحُرٍ مَّا نَفِدَتْ كَلِمَاتُ اللَّهِ ۗ إِنَّ اللَّهَ عَزِيزٌ حَكِيمٌ

tainers. These are numbers that are literally beyond our imagination; our minds can't comprehend them.

Regarding this example, Syed Quṭb ﷺ writes, "This scene is taken straight from people's limited knowledge and observations, but aims to put before them the meaning of God's ever-renewing will which is neither limited nor restrained. Their minds cannot visualize this concept without such a comparison. People record their knowledge and speeches, and sign their orders, using pens, which used to be made of reed, and ink which hardly filled an inkpot or a bottle. The comparison drawn here shows them that if all the trees on earth were made into pens, and all the seas were made into ink this would still be insufficient to describe God's inexhaustible might. Furthermore, even if this sea of ink was given supplies with seven more seas, while scribes sat to record God's words that speak of His knowledge and will, it would still be insufficient. All the pens, ink, trees and seas will be used up and exhausted, while God's words will not end. It is a case where what is finite is faced with the infinite. No matter how huge the finite is, it will come to an end, while the infinite remains undiminished. God's words will not finish, not ever, because His knowledge is unlimited and His will unrestricted. Trees, seas, living creatures, objects, and situations all come to an end. The human heart stands in awe before God's majesty, which is endless, unchanging: "God is indeed Almighty, Wise." [193]

We as human beings should never be deceived or fooled by our own intellect and abilities. No matter how much we learn and how advanced we become scientifically and technologically, it's nothing compared to the infinite knowledge and wisdom of Allah ﷻ. Our knowledge compared to the knowledge of Allah ﷻ is like a drop of water compared to all the oceans. Allah ﷻ then ends the noble Sūrah by reminding the Prophet ﷺ about humility and us about the path of true salvation.

193 Quṭb, *fī Ẓilāl al-Quran*, 4:2296-2297

VERSE 110

قُلْ إِنَّمَا أَنَا بَشَرٌ مِّثْلُكُمْ يُوحَىٰ إِلَيَّ أَنَّمَا إِلَٰهُكُمْ إِلَٰهٌ وَاحِدٌ ۖ
فَمَن كَانَ يَرْجُو لِقَاءَ رَبِّهِ فَلْيَعْمَلْ عَمَلًا صَالِحًا وَلَا يُشْرِكْ
بِعِبَادَةِ رَبِّهِ أَحَدًا ﴿١١٠﴾

110 Say, "I am only a human being like you. It has been revealed to me that your God is one God. So whosoever hopes for the meeting with his Lord, let him perform righteous deeds and make no one a partner with his Lord in worship.

In this verse, Allah ﷻ is speaking directly to the Prophet ﷺ. He ﷻ is telling him to tell his people, his community, that he is a human being just like them. He's not an Angel nor is he divine in any way, shape, or form. He eats, drinks, walks, talks and sleeps just like any other human being. The only difference is that he has been selected and chosen as a Prophet and Messenger who receives revelation from the Most High ﷻ. Part of what has been revealed to him is that there is only one God, alone without any partners and that whoever believes in the meeting with their Lord, meaning they believe in the last day, resurrection, accountability, and judgment, they know that the life of this world is temporary and finite and that the life of the hereafter is eternal and infinite, should "perform righteous deeds and make no one a partner with his Lord in worship."

"Righteous deeds" include fulfilling all of our obligations, obeying the commands of Allah ﷻ and staying away from His prohibitions. It includes all voluntary acts of worship such as praying, fasting, reading Quran, making dua, dhikr, and charity. It includes being kind to our parents, spouses, children, relatives, neighbors, and co-workers. It even includes smiling at someone. There are multiple paths of righteousness in Islam.

We're then reminded to not associate partners with Allah ﷻ in our worship; to not commit shirk. Several commentators mention that shirk here refers to ostentation; performing righteous deeds in order to show off. There are two types of shirk: al-shirk al-akbar (the greater shirk) and al-shirk al-aṣghar (the smaller shrik). al-Shirk al-Akbar is associating partners with Allah ﷻ; it's an act of disbelief, which will be discussed shortly. al-Shirk al-Aṣghar refers to ostentation and showing off or not having sincerity in acts of worship. The Prophet ﷺ referred to ostentation as "the lesser idolatry." The Prophet ﷺ said, "I do not fear that you will worship the sun, the stars and the moon, but I fear your worshipping other than Allah through ostentation." The Prophet ﷺ said, "What I fear most for my community is doing things for other than the sake of Allah."[194]

The word for ostentation in Arabic is الرِّيَاء. It's derived from the root letters ر أ ى that convey the meaning of looking or showing. al-Riyā' literally means to do something to show off; to show to others. al-Jurjānī ؒ defined it as leaving sincerity in one's actions by being concerned with someone other than Allah.[195] In simpler words, it is doing something with the purpose of catching the attention and praise of others. It is considered to be a destructive disease of the heart and its root cause is described as wanting something from a source other than Allah ﷻ. Imām al-Ghazālī ؒ writes that the cure for ostentation is to actively and sincerely seek purification of the heart by removing four things:

1. Love of praise
2. Fear of blame
3. Desire for worldly benefit from people, and
4. Fear of harm from people

al-Ḥasan ؒ was asked about sincerity and ostentation. He said, "An aspect of sincerity is to love that your good deeds be concealed, and to not love that your bad deeds be concealed. If Allah ﷻ exposes your good deeds say, 'This is from your favor and grace and is not my own doing,' and re-

194 ibn Mājah, *k. al-zuhd*, 4205

195 Al-Jurjānī, *al-Taʿrīfāt*, p 119

member the statement of Allah ﷻ, 'So whosoever hopes for the meeting with his Lord, let him perform righteous deeds and make no one a partner with his Lord in worship.' 'Those who give whatever they give', they give sincerely while fearing that it won't be accepted from them. As for ostentation, then it is to seek a soul's share from this world." Someone asked him, "How can this be?" He said, "Whoever seeks something other than Allah ﷻ and the hereafter through their action, it is ostentation."[196]

According to several sources, this portion of the verse was revealed in response to a companion that came to the Prophet ﷺ seeking clarity regarding sincerity, intentions, and acceptance. A man came to the Prophet ﷺ and said, "O Messenger of Allah ﷺ, I perform deeds for Allah ﷻ seeking His pleasure. However, when someone finds out about it it makes me happy. The Prophet ﷺ said, "Truly Allah ﷻ is pure and only accepts that which is pure. He doesn't accept that which He has been made a partner in."[197] The Prophet ﷺ is explaining to the Companion the importance of sincerity and that in order for an act to be accepted by Allah ﷻ the intention behind it must be pure. In another version, a man came to the Prophet ﷺ and said, "O Messenger of Allah ﷺ! I give charity and maintain a good relationship with my relatives only for the sake of Allah ﷻ. Then this is mentioned about me and I am praised for it and it makes me happy." The Messenger of Allah ﷺ remained silent and Allah ﷻ revealed, "So whosoever hopes for the meeting with his Lord, let him perform righteous deeds and make no one a partner with his Lord in worship."[198]

The cornerstone of sound belief, the foundation and main pillar of our entire system of belief, is that Allah ﷻ alone is the Creator and Master of the entire heavens and the earth and whatever they contain. He alone is the Originator, Creator, Fashioner, Sustainer, Provider, Sovereign, Owner, the Almighty, the All Wise. Allah ﷻ alone is the One who bestows blessings and favors and He is the only being worthy and deserving of worship. To believe that Allah ﷻ is absolutely unique; nothing in this universe resembles Him in any way, shape, or form.

Oneness is one of the divine attributes of Allah ﷻ; He is unique in terms of His essence, attributes, and actions. What that means is that there is no

---

196 Qurṭubī, *al-Jāmiʿ fī Aḥkām al-Quran*, 13:400

197 Qurṭubī, *al-Jāmiʿ fī Aḥkām al-Quran*, 13:398

198 Qurṭubī, *al-Jāmiʿ fī Aḥkām al-Quran*, 13:398

deity besides Allah ﷻ, the likeness of His attributes are not found in any other being, and that no one can act independently of Him and no one has a share in His actions. No one should take anyone or anything besides Allah ﷻ as an object of worship. It is absurd to assign divinity to any person or object besides Allah ﷻ.

Allah ﷻ describes doing so as the greatest form of injustice. When a person commits shirk they're directing their worship to the wrong place and they're equating creation to the Creator. The word shirk literally means to "associate partners." Technically it means to accept that there are deities equal to Allah ﷻ in His names, attributes, and actions. Those who commit shirk don't deny the existence of Allah ﷻ, but they believe in other gods that have similar names, attributes, will, and in terms of authority are equivalent to and have the same powers as Allah ﷻ and therefore worship them.

Now, rationally speaking, associating partners with Allah ﷻ is absurd and doesn't make sense. How can a created being or object be equal to the Creator? How can something that can't cause harm or bring benefit be equal to Allah? It is considered to be the greatest of major sins and a great injustice because it is a violation of the exclusive right of Allah ﷻ. It is belittling the might, power, magnificence, glory and greatness of God. For some of us it may be difficult to understand why committing shirk is such a great offence. That is because we have this "notion that wrongs must have a discernible victim. But in Islam, we recognize not only the rights of man, but, more importantly, the rights of God. God's rights are inviolable and non-negotiable."

Within the framework of Islam we acknowledge and recognize two sets of rights:

1. The rights of man and
2. The rights of Allah ﷻ

If we violate the rights of man, it seems tangible and we know that we have to make up for it in some way. There are consequences in this world as well. However, when we violate the rights of Allah ﷻ, it may seem a little intangible because the consequences of doing so will be fully experienced in the hereafter. And as mentioned above, the rights of Allah ﷻ in terms of belief and worship are inviolable and non-negotiable.

Allah ﷻ is the One who created us, fashioned us, provides and sustains us, bestows countless blessings and favors, and in response someone refuses to believe in Him or associates partners with Him. That is an affront to Allah ﷻ and that is why it is described as a major injustice.

This brings us to then end of this noble and beautiful Sūrah, Sūrah al-Kahf, a Sūrah that has a special and unique status because the Prophet ﷺ encouraged us to recite it specifically on Fridays. Through four stories, the Sūrah focuses on four different types of trials we're going to face in this world and how to respond to them. To recap:

1.

The story of the people of the cave represents the trial of faith. And we're taught that one of the best ways to deal with it is through good company; surrounding ourselves with people of faith and righteousness.

2.

The story of the owner of the two gardens is representative of the trial of wealth. We're taught the most powerful way to deal with it is by recognizing the reality of the life of this world.

3.

The story of Musa ﷷ with al-Khaḍir is representative of the trial of knowledge and the way to deal with it is through seeking knowledge and humility.

4.

The last story, the story of Dhū al-Qarnayn, is representative of the trial of power. The solution is sincerity and righteousness.

All thanks and praise are for Allah ﷻ and may His salutations and blessings be upon His last and final Messenger, Muḥammad ﷺ.

BIBLIOGRAPHY

al-Ālūsī, Maḥmūd ibn Abd Allah. *Rūh al-Maʿānī fī Tafsīr al-Quran al-ʿAẓīm wa al-Sabʿ al-Mathānī*. Beirut: Mu'assasah al-Risālah, 2010

al-Baghawī, al-Ḥussain ibn Masūd. *Maʿālim al-Tanzīl*. Saudi Arabia: Dār al-Ṭayyibah, 2010

al-Gharnāṭī, Muḥammad ibn Yūsuf. *al-Baḥr al-Muḥīṭ fī al-Tafsīr*. Makkah: al-Maktabah al-Tijāriyyah

al-Maẓharī, Muḥammad Thanā Allah. *al-Tafsīr al-Maẓharī*. Beirut: Dār al-Kutub al-Ilmiyyah, 2007

al-Qurṭubī, Muḥammad ibn Aḥmad. *al-Jāmiʿ lī Aḥkām al-Quran*. Damascus: Mu'assasah al-Risālah, 2013

al-Rāzī, Fakhr al-Dīn. *Mafātīḥ al-Ghayb*. Cairo: Dār al-Ḥadīth, 2012

al-Shawkānī, Muḥammad ibn Alī. *Fatḥ al-Qadīr*. Beirut: Dār ibn Ḥazm, 2005

al-Ṭabarī, Muḥammad ibn Jarīr. *Jāmiʿ al-Bayān ʿan Ta'wīl Āyy al-Quran*. Beirut: Dār ibn Ḥazm, 2013

al-Zūḥailī, Wahbah. *al-Tafsīr al-Munīr fī al-ʿAqīdah wa al-Sharīʿah wa al-Manhaj*. Damascus: Dār al-Fikr, 2009

ibn Āshūr, Muḥammad al-Ṭāhir. *Tafsīr al-Taḥrīr wa al-Tanwīr*. Beirut:

Mu'assasah al-Tārīkh

Ibn Kathīr, Ismāīl. *Tafsīr al-Quran al-ʿAẓīm*. Saudi Arabia: Dār Ālam al-Kutub, 2004

Quṭb, Syed. *fī Ẓilāl al-Quran*. Cairo: Dār al-Shurūq, 2009

Shafi, Muhammad. *Maʿriful Qur'an*. Pakistan: Maktaba-e-Darul-Uloom, 2003

Made in the USA
Coppell, TX
27 February 2026